Approaches to learning and teaching

Primary

a toolkit for international teachers

Tony Cotton

Series Editors: Paul Ellis and Lauren Harris

CAMBRIDGE
UNIVERSITY PRESS

University Printing House, Cambridge CB2 8BS, United Kingdom

One Liberty Plaza, 20th Floor, New York, NY 10006, USA

477 Williamstown Road, Port Melbourne, VIC 3207, Australia

314–321, 3rd Floor, Plot 3, Splendor Forum, Jasola District Centre, New Delhi – 110025, India

79 Anson Road, #06–04/06, Singapore 079906

Cambridge University Press is part of the University of Cambridge.

It furthers the University's mission by disseminating knowledge in the pursuit of education, learning and research at the highest international levels of excellence.

www.cambridge.org
Information on this title: www.cambridge.org/9781108436953 (Paperback)

© Cambridge Assessment International Education 2018

® IGCSE is a registered trademark

First published 2018

20 19 18 17 16 15 14 13 12 11 10 9 8 7 6 5 4

Printed in Great Britain by CPI Group (UK) Ltd, Croydon CR0 4YY

A catalogue record for this publication is available from the British Library

ISBN 978-1-108-43695-3 Paperback

Contents

Online lesson ideas for this book can be found at
cambridge.org/9781108436953

Acknowledgements

The authors and publishers acknowledge the following sources of copyright material and are grateful for the permissions granted. While every effort has been made, it has not always been possible to identify the sources of all the material used, or to trace all copyright holders. If any omissions are brought to our notice, we will be happy to include the appropriate acknowledgements on reprinting.

Cover image: bgblue/Getty Images; Fig 3.1 Bettman/Getty Images; Fig 3.3 Heritage Images/Hulton Archive/Getty Images; Fig 4.2 Ignasi Soler/Alamy Stock Photo; Fig 6.1 Underwood Archives/Archive Photos/Getty Images; Fig 6.2 Eco Images/Universal Images Group/ Getty Images; Fig 6.3 classroom designs used by permission of Mercer Hall and Patricia Russac, The American Society For Innovation Design In Education, 2012; Fig 9.2 *Talking Maths, Talking Languages*. The Association of Teachers of Mathematics; Fig 9.3 Sally and Richard Greenhill /Alamy Stock Photo; lesson idea 6.3 Keystone/Hulton Archive/Getty Images; lesson idea 9.1 Adekvat/iStock/Getty Images, Ylivdesign/Getty Images; Fig 12.1 and lesson idea 12.2 Graphics from 'The World of 100' by Toby Ng (www.toby-ng.com) used with permission

I would like to thank Cambridge University Press for asking me to contribute to this series. I am delighted that the series editors have recognised the importance of the early phases of learning.

I would also like to thank Jane Wood who acted as development editor on this book. Her diligence means that what you see before you is readable!

The commitment of teachers in international schools to the development of all learners through education is what inspires me, so thanks are due to all the teachers I have worked with around the globe.

Finally, I must acknowledge the two people who are currently teaching me most about learning: my beautiful grandsons, Tate and Felix.

Introduction to the series by the editors

1

1 Approaches to learning and teaching Primary

This series of books is the result of close collaboration between Cambridge University Press and Cambridge Assessment International Education, both departments of the University of Cambridge. The books are intended as a companion guide for teachers, to supplement your learning and provide you with extra resources for the lessons you are planning. Their focus is deliberately not syllabus-specific, although occasional reference has been made to programmes and qualifications. We want to invite you to set aside for a while assessment objectives and grading, and take the opportunity instead to look in more depth at how you teach your subject and how you motivate and engage with your students.

The themes presented in these books are informed by evidence-based research into what works to improve students' learning and pedagogical best practices. To ensure that these books are first and foremost practical resources, we have chosen not to include too many academic references, but we have provided some suggestions for further reading.

We have further enhanced the books by asking the authors to create accompanying lesson ideas. These are described in the text and can be found in a dedicated space online. We hope the books will become a dynamic and valid representation of what is happening now in learning and teaching in the context in which you work.

Our organisations also offer a wide range of professional development opportunities for teachers. These range from syllabus- and topic-specific workshops and large-scale conferences to suites of accredited qualifications for teachers and school leaders. Our aim is to provide you with valuable support, to build communities and networks, and to help you both enrich your own teaching methodology and evaluate its impact on your students.

Each of the books in this series follows a similar structure. In the third chapter, we have asked our authors to consider the essential elements of their subject, the main concepts that might be covered in a school curriculum, and why these are important. The next chapters give you a brief guide on how to interpret a syllabus or subject guide, and how to plan a programme of study. The authors will encourage you to think too about what is not contained in a syllabus and how you can pass on your own passion for the subject you teach.

The main body of the text takes you through those aspects of learning and teaching which are widely recognised as important. We would like to stress that there is no single recipe for excellent teaching, and that different schools, operating in different countries and cultures, will have strong traditions that should be respected. There is a growing consensus, however, about some important practices and approaches that need to be adopted if students are going to fulfil their potential and be prepared for modern life.

In the common introduction to each of these chapters, we look at what the research says and the benefits and challenges of particular approaches. Each author then focuses on how to translate theory into practice in the context of their subject, offering practical lesson ideas and teacher tips. These chapters are not mutually exclusive but can be read independently of each other and in whichever order suits you best. They form a coherent whole but are presented in such a way that you can dip into the book when and where it is most convenient for you to do so.

The final two chapters are common to all the books in this series and are not written by the subject authors. After the subject context chapters, we include guidance on how to reflect on your teaching and some avenues you might explore to develop your own professional learning. Schools and educational organisations are increasingly interested in the impact that classroom practice has on student outcomes. We have therefore included an exploration of this topic and some practical advice on how to evaluate the success of the learning opportunities you are providing for your students.

We hope you find these books accessible and useful. We have tried to make them conversational in tone so you feel we are sharing good practice rather than directing it. Above all, we hope that the books will inspire you and enable you to think in more depth about how you teach and how your students learn.

Paul Ellis and Lauren Harris

Series Editors

2 | Purpose and context

International research into educational effectiveness tells us that student achievement is influenced most by what teachers do in classrooms. In a world of rankings and league tables we tend to notice performance, not preparation, yet the product of education is more than just examinations and certification. Education is also about the formation of effective learning habits that are crucial for success within and beyond the taught curriculum.

The purpose of this series of books is to inspire you as a teacher to reflect on your practice, try new approaches and better understand how to help your students learn. We aim to help you develop your teaching so that your students are prepared for the next level of their education as well as life in the modern world.

This book will encourage you to examine the processes of learning and teaching, not just the outcomes. We will explore a variety of teaching strategies to enable you to select which is most appropriate for your students and the context in which you teach. When you are making your choice, involve your students: all the ideas presented in this book will work best if you engage your students, listen to what they have to say, and consistently evaluate their needs.

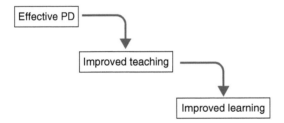

Cognitive psychologists, coaches and sports writers have noted how the aggregation of small changes can lead to success at the highest level. As teachers, we can help our students make marginal gains by guiding them in their learning, encouraging them to think and talk about how they are learning, and giving them the tools to monitor their success. If you take care of the learning, the performance will take care of itself.

When approaching an activity for the first time, or revisiting an area of learning, ask yourself if your students know how to:

- approach a new task and plan which strategies they will use
- monitor their progress and adapt their approach if necessary
- look back and reflect on how well they did and what they might do differently next time.

Approaches to learning and teaching Primary

Effective students understand that learning is an active process. We need to challenge and stretch our students and enable them to interrogate, analyse and evaluate what they see and hear. Consider whether your students:

- challenge assumptions and ask questions
- try new ideas and take intellectual risks
- devise strategies to overcome any barriers to their learning that they encounter.

As we discuss in Chapter 6 **Active learning** and Chapter 8 **Metacognition**, it is our role as teachers to encourage these practices with our students so that they become established routines. We can help students review their own progress as well as getting a snapshot ourselves of how far they are progressing by using some of the methods we explore in Chapter 7 on **Assessment for Learning**.

Students often view the subject lessons they are attending as separate from each other, but they can gain a great deal if we encourage them to take a more holistic appreciation of what they are learning. This requires not only understanding how various concepts in a subject fit together, but also how to make connections between different areas of knowledge and how to transfer skills from one discipline to another. As our students successfully integrate disciplinary knowledge, they are better able to solve complex problems, generate new ideas and interpret the world around them.

In order for students to construct an understanding of the world and their significance in it, we need to lead students into thinking habitually about why a topic is important on a personal, local and global scale. Do they realise the implications of what they are learning and what they do with their knowledge and skills, not only for themselves but also for their neighbours and the wider world? To what extent can they recognise and express their own perspective as well as the perspectives of others? We will consider how to foster local and global awareness, as well as personal and social responsibility, in Chapter 12 on **Global thinking**.

As part of the learning process, some students will discover barriers to their learning: we need to recognise these and help students to overcome them. Even students who regularly meet success face their own challenges. We have all experienced barriers to our own learning at some point in our lives and should be able as teachers to empathise and share our own methods for dealing with these.

In Chapter 10 **Inclusive education** we discuss how to make learning accessible for everyone and how to ensure that all students receive the instruction and support they need to succeed as students.

Some students are learning through the medium of English when it is not their first language, while others may struggle to understand subject jargon even if they might otherwise appear fluent. For all students, whether they are learning through their first language or an additional language, language is a vehicle for learning. It is through language that students access the content of the lesson and communicate their ideas. So, as teachers, it is our responsibility to make sure that language isn't a barrier to learning. In Chapter 9 on **Language awareness** we look at how teachers can pay closer attention to language to ensure that all students can access the content of a lesson.

Alongside a greater understanding of what works in education and why, we (as teachers) can also seek to improve how we teach and expand the tools we have at our disposal. For this reason, we have included Chapter 11 **Teaching with digital technologies**, discussing what this means for our classrooms and for us as teachers. Institutes of higher education and employers want to work with students who are effective communicators and who are information literate. Technology brings both advantages and challenges and we invite you to reflect on how to use it appropriately.

This book has been written to help you think harder about the impact of your teaching on your students' learning. It is up to you to set an example for your students and to provide them with opportunities to celebrate success, learn from failure and, ultimately, to succeed.

We hope you will share what you gain from this book with other teachers and that you will be inspired by the ideas that are presented here. We hope that you will encourage your school leaders to foster a positive environment that allows both you and your students to meet with success and to learn from mistakes when success is not immediate. We hope too that this book can help in the creation and continuation of a culture where learning and teaching are valued and through which we can discover together what works best for each and every one of our students.

3 | The nature of the subject

Introduction

Primary teachers often say that they chose to teach younger children as they want to teach children and not a subject. While primary teachers do have particular interests in particular subject areas, they often describe themselves as generalists rather than specialists. Being a generalist brings with it a challenge: understanding how young children learn while at the same time understanding enough about each separate subject to enthuse and inspire learners in every area.

Key theories: Piaget and Vygotsky

Many primary teachers who have undertaken a course of teacher education will have been introduced to the educational theories of Piaget and Vygotsky, both cognitive psychologists who explored how children learn. Their ideas underpin much of what is now taken for granted as good practice in learning and teaching in the primary school. While psychologists of the mind explored how children learn, their ideas have been drawn on to develop teaching approaches suitable for primary classrooms.

Piagetian theory

Piaget (Figure 3.1) suggested that young learners construct their own understanding of the world around them based on their own interactions with the world. They develop schemas through repetitive actions or playful activities which in turn become building blocks of knowledge. They can use these building blocks to create mental models of the world. You may have noticed a child repeating an action to see if the outcome remains the same. For example, they open a door and notice that the draught from the door means that a balloon blows across the floor. They smile, close the door, move the balloon back to the door and try again. The same thing happens. They repeat a further time.

Figure 3.1: Jean Piaget (1896–1980).

The next morning they may try once more just to check. They now understand the cause and effect.

Another of Piaget's models describes the process of assimilation and accommodation. This is a process through which learners come to new knowledge.

- Assimilation: we currently see the world according to schemas we have developed.
- Accommodation: we notice something that does not fit our current schema. This is sometimes called 'cognitive conflict'.
- Equilibration: we redevelop our schema to take account of our new learning.

An example from Mathematics would be a learner who has only ever experienced multiplication by integers (whole numbers). They may have developed the schema, 'Multiplication always makes a number larger'. They are then introduced to the calculation $7 \times 0.5 = 3.5$. At first this seems uncomfortable. There is a sense of 'disequilibrium'. The world of multiplication has become shaky. Their teacher shows them the image in Figure 3.2, illustrating seven 'lots of' one half.

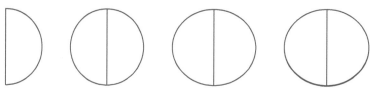

Figure 3.2: Visual representation of 7 x 0.5.

As they understand multiplication as repeated addition, learners can now assimilate this new knowledge.

Teacher Tip

Always ask learners to articulate their thinking. Ask them why they have given you an answer or ask them to try to explain their thinking. In this way, you will begin to understand the schemas that they are developing.

☑ LESSON IDEA ONLINE 3.1: ODD ONE OUT

Use this lesson idea to help develop learners' skills in articulating their thinking.

Another key theory of Piaget was his theory of stages of development. He suggested that children move through four stages of cognitive development. He did not attach these to ages, although ages are often attributed to each stage.

1   The sensorimotor stage – this means a child can form a mental representation of an object.
2   The preoperational stage – at this stage children can think symbolically. They understand that a symbol can stand for something other than itself.
3   The concrete operational stage – at this stage children can internalise their thinking and do not need to use concrete objects to try things out.
4   The formal operational stage – at this stage learners can think about abstract concepts and test hypotheses to develop their schemas.

It is important not to see these stages as fixed. For example, I know of many adults who will make models to help them think through new ideas. We should perhaps see them as stages of learning new things, rather than stages that are attached to all learning at a particular age.

Vygotskian theory

Vygotsky (Figure 3.3) believed that all learning stemmed from social interactions; that is, we learn through communicating with others. Two main principles of his work are the 'more knowledgeable other' (MKO)

Figure 3.3: Lev Vygotsky (1896–1934).

and the zone of proximal development (ZPD). Vygotskian theory suggests that we all learn through drawing on the skills of someone (or something – a book, a piece of software) who has greater experience than us in the area we are studying. This is our MKO.

The ZPD is the difference between what a child could achieve independently and what they could achieve with the support of an MKO (Table 3.1).

Zone of Proximal Development		
What is already known	What can be understood with guidance and support from an MKO	What is not known

Table 3.1

Teacher Tip

Vary the ways that you group your learners. They can act as MKOs for each other, so it is important to have learners with different prior experience and understanding working together.

What makes an effective primary teacher?

In 2016, the Teaching Schools Council in the UK released a report titled 'Effective Primary Teaching Practice' (available from the Teaching Schools Council website).

This very thorough report included an analysis of what makes an effective primary teacher, and suggested it was much more than simply understanding a subject. The authors suggested that teachers require:

- an understanding of the key concepts of the subject to be taught
- knowledge of the ways in which learners might progress through these key concepts
- knowledge of the misconceptions that learners may have (this relates back to Piaget earlier)
- a range of strategies so that they can plan the most appropriate activities for their group of learners.

As primary teachers, there will be some areas of the curriculum in which we feel secure and others in which we are less confident. This report would suggest that to become effective across the whole curriculum, teachers need to work hard to develop subject knowledge in areas in which we feel less confident.

The aims of primary education

There are many curricula around the world and they often begin with a statement of aims. The school that you work with may well subscribe to a curriculum which has clearly stated aims, or the teachers in the school may have developed aims for themselves. It is important that you understand what these aims are and that you can apply them in your teaching. One way to do this is to find the statement of aims and think about lessons that you have taught in two or three different subject disciplines recently. Ask yourself, 'To what extent did my teaching meet these aims?' If you did not meet these aims through your teaching, ask yourself, 'What might I have done differently to ensure I met the aims?'

Teacher Tip

Display the school aims, or the aims of the curriculum that your school follows, on the classroom wall. Ask learners to evaluate how effectively they think a particular lesson meets the aims. Agree how the lesson could be developed to better meet the aims. In this way, the aims will make more sense to learners and to you.

To develop aims for your school, you may like to consider these questions:

- What makes an educated person?
- What sort of teachers can best develop an educated person?
- How can the whole school community support the development of educated people?
- What do you hope a young person will gain from your teaching by the time they leave your primary school?
- What skills, abilities and understanding will they have?

Then consider the types of activities and experiences they will need to have during their time in primary school to develop these skills, abilities and understanding.

Key challenges for teaching in the primary school

There are many challenges for primary school teachers. You will certainly be able to develop your own list. My personal list would include:

- assessing learning so that pupils and teachers know what is understood and what the next stage of learning should be
- planning for differentiation so that all pupils can access the curriculum and move forward in their understanding
- planning across the whole curriculum
- ensuring the holistic development of pupils through after-school clubs, experiences outside the classroom or learning from others who come into school to offer alternative learning experiences
- being expected to improve results in external examinations every year even though cohorts of children vary.

I aim to meet these challenges by:

- ensuring that I understand the assessment data that is available at an individual level – in that way, I can ensure that each learner achieves their potential
- developing my strategies for Assessment for Learning (see Chapter 7 **Assessment for Learning**)
- ensuring that I adopt an inclusive approach to learning and teaching (see Chapter 10 **Inclusive education**)
- ensuring that I make links between different curriculum areas whenever possible – learners don't experience the world in subject boxes out of school so it is important to teach through cross-curricular experiences whenever possible
- developing networks within the extended school community so that I can use the skills available in the wider community.

The last two bullet points above describe the challenge of working in a cross-curricular way. Lesson idea 3.2 shows how links can be made between literacy and Science. In some countries the focus in the earliest years of education is on developing language and literacy. I would argue that it is more effective to develop language and literacy skills across the curriculum.

☑ LESSON IDEA ONLINE 3.2: BUILD A FLYING MACHINE
This lesson idea explores properties of materials using a story book.

Whatever challenges you face, the most effective way to meet a challenge is to find an ally. The most useful piece of advice ever given to me was to find a colleague on the staff to collaborate with; someone who shared my beliefs and values; someone whose advice I could draw on and someone who would support me when I needed support. Teaching in the primary classroom is challenging by its very nature, but, through working closely with colleagues, you will find it incredibly rewarding.

Summary

In this chapter, we have explored:

- the key theories of learning developed by Piaget and Vygotsky and how these ideas apply to teaching in the primary classroom

- key aims for teaching in the primary classroom

- how to meet the challenges you will face in your teaching.

4 | Key considerations

Introduction

Any group of teachers around the world is likely to have a shared sense of how a classroom should look, of how a teacher should teach and of what shape the curriculum might take. However, it is important not just to repeat approaches that we experienced as learners. Before focusing on pedagogy or curriculum, primary teachers need to consider the values and beliefs that underpin education. Start by asking why we structure education in a particular way, why we choose a particular teaching approach and why the learners we work with have particular expectations of us as their teachers. In this chapter I will discuss how to share your expertise in a primary setting, explore a variety of resources in your teaching and illustrate challenges pupils face in their learning.

Two stories will illustrate how the diversity of experience from around the world can benefit us all by broadening our perspective. The first concerns a group of primary teachers from Scandinavia working among an international group of teachers. The Scandinavian teachers expected to work with the same group of learners from the age of five to the age of fourteen. This amazed some of the other teachers. 'What if you have a bad relationship with one of the learners?' they asked. 'It must be terrible to think that you have to work with this learner for the next eight years.' The Scandinavian teachers looked confused. 'We make sure that we develop positive relationships with all the learners,' they said. The system they were a part of meant that they looked at relationships with learners in a very different way from some of their international counterparts.

The second story involves a group of teachers from Portugal, sharing experiences about grouping practices. Primary schools in some other countries at the time were differentiating lessons by offering separate activities to 'target groups' based on prior attainment. The Portuguese colleagues found this very strange. 'So, you place children in different groups and these groups will not all be able to reach the same level of attainment?' they asked. 'We would not be able to do this – the parents would be angry if they thought that their children were not being offered the same possibilities for progression as all the other students.' I offer these stories not to judge one system against another but to suggest that there is no such thing as normal in the primary classroom.

Share your expertise

All primary teachers have expertise in a particular curriculum area. Sometimes teachers are a little bashful about showing this expertise. I once worked with a teacher who was in one of the finest brass bands in his country. I asked him if he had ever played for his class. He said, 'No – I don't want to show off.' I persuaded him to bring in his tuba and he performed for us all. His class sat spellbound. They were incredibly proud of their teacher and several of them talked about instruments they were learning. Others excitedly discussed the instruments they would like to play. You could sense a shift in the relationship. The learners were more motivated to learn from this teacher because they now saw him as an expert. He didn't have to be an expert in everything; being an expert in one area was enough to inspire them. So if you are an artist, share your sketchbook and portfolio with your learners. If you are a historian, talk about your favourite period. If you are a scientist, discuss areas that particularly interest you, and if you are a mathematician, share mathematical problems you are working on and talk to the learners about them.

Working as a team

You cannot be an expert in every subject area. You cannot possibly know everything. This means that to cover all curriculum areas, planning with others is very important. This has the additional advantage of cutting down on your planning time. Offer to share planning with another teacher you enjoy working with. You may have a particular interest in Science and your colleague may be a Geographer. This offers two possibilities. You can plan the Science inputs for them and they can plan the Geography inputs for you. You can both teach the same lesson and then discuss how effective the lessons were with your two classes. Or you can plan a cross-curricular unit exploring Science and Geography.

Revel in ignorance

Very early in my career, a learner asked me: 'Who invented the typewriter?' 'Sylvie Typewriter,' I said, covering my embarrassment with humour. The learner was not impressed. I felt useless because I didn't know the answer. Then I realised that I could not be expected to know everything. That evening I carried out some research and discovered that a very early 'typewriter' was used as early as the 16th century. I became interested and the next day sought out the learner to share the new information and my excitement at what I had discovered.

A colleague who teaches drama once used the phrase 'revelling in ignorance' to describe that moment when we realise that we don't know something and that this opens up the possibilities for learning. We should be excited when we discover that we don't know something as this means that we are about to find out something new.

Model wanting to learn

An important part of being a pupil in a primary school is that they are learning how to learn. We learn how to learn by observing someone else learning, and by learning alongside them. This means that if teachers put themselves in the position of being a pupil in the classroom, their class will observe and try to mimic the learning behaviours. One way to motivate pupils at the start of a new topic is to begin the exploration for yourself before they enter the room. As they come in they will ask, 'What are you doing?' You can explain what you are investigating and it is very likely that they will want to join the investigation.

Teacher Tip

While the pupils are out of the classroom, place a large piece of paper in one corner of the room. Begin to explore an open-ended mathematical investigation (see Figure 4.1) by jotting on this piece of paper. As the children return to the room, explain the investigation to them and the progress you are making. Invite them to contribute to your investigation on the large sheet of paper which they can then take away to continue the investigation.

An open-ended investigation

Roll a spinner. Write down the number.

If it is an odd number, multiply it by 3 and add 1.

If it is an even number, divide it by 2.

Follow these rules to create a chain. Keep going until you reach 1.

Choose any one or two digit number and create new chains.

Join up chains that contain the same number.

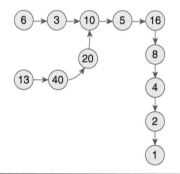

Figure 4.1: An open-ended maths investigation.

What resources should I use?

We should not interpret resources simply as books or other physical objects. Primary teachers can draw on a wide range of other resources. The most important resource in a school is people. I discussed the importance of calling on other teachers as a resource in the section 'Share your expertise'. Similarly we can draw on a range of other adults who are members of the wider school community. These might be parents or carers who work in particular jobs that have relevance to the curriculum, or artists or other creatives who can support you in creative work.

Other adults (including parents)

Parents are a wonderful resource. Many parents are willing to be involved in their child's education. Some parents and grandparents have skills or experiences that will be extremely valuable to you. Perhaps you are covering a period in history which a grandparent experienced or has photographs of. If you are studying a particular industrial process or scientific idea, you may have a parent who can talk about how this relates to their work. There may be artists, textile workers, town planners or architects available to you. Find out what resources of this kind exist in the school community.

Teacher Tip

When you are exploring the nature of the number system, use all the languages and scripts that are used by parents or grandparents. Looking at unfamiliar systems helps us see the patterns in the system we are more used to.

Similarly, share reading books in all the languages available to your class. Ask parents and grandparents to lead these multilingual reading sessions to draw on their skills in languages that you are unfamiliar with.

Subject-specific resources

I recently visited a primary school which had introduced the use of Cuisenaire® rods across the whole school as the main manipulative to develop mathematical thinking. These rods were devised in the 1950s by a Belgian, Georges Cuisenaire, and popularised by an Egyptian mathematician working in the UK, Caleb Gattegno. They are starting to be used more widely again in English schools. I visited this school early in the first term when the young pupils had just been given their own set of rods.

Figure 4.2: Cuisenaire rods.

These rods are labelled with each child's name and are theirs to keep for the next six years of their education. This sends an important message to the learners. First, learning can be supported by the use of manipulatives; they are not simply something to be used in the early years of primary education. Second, learning is a long-term business. Something that you learn early in your educational career will be used as you progress through the school.

The outdoors and the environment at home

The outdoor environment or the home environment of your learners are sometimes underused resources. There are many occasions when your teaching can be enriched by using examples from the outdoor environment. If you are studying the weather, consider carrying out weather observations over a period of weeks outside. Similarly you can enrich History studies by visiting a museum, or biology by observing wildlife in the local environment.

> ☑ **LESSON IDEA ONLINE 4.1: CLASSIFYING MATERIALS**
> This lesson explores classifying a concept which is important to both Science and Mathematics.

What challenges do learners face?

Emotions and relationships

Young learners face many challenges at school. Probably the biggest challenge is adapting to the institution of education and to schooling while learning how to handle their emotional development. Relationships and friendships are central to all our experiences. All teachers know that when these relationships are strained, young learners find it difficult to learn anything. Learning is an emotional experience and developing as a young person is also emotional. We cannot banish emotions from the classroom.

☑ **LESSON IDEA ONLINE 4.2: SELF-ESTEEM SHIELD**
This lesson offers an example of how we can support learners in developing emotional intelligence.

Motivation

Very young children are curious. They are intrinsically motivated to learn. They want to discover how the world around them operates. However, they do not follow a curriculum. Their learning follows whichever path interests them at the time. As pupils progress through primary school, they come to understand that there has to be a balance of following their own interest and having to follow a set curriculum. As they grow older, the curriculum tends to take over and pupils need to develop extrinsic motivation; that is, a motivation to 'do well', to be successful for the affirmation of someone whose opinion they value, or to be successful against some form of external measure.

Tensions between home and school

Some learners may experience tensions between home and school. The expectations of how children learn may be different between home and school. Parents' and carers' expectations will be based on their own experience of education, which may be very different from their child's experience. Private tutors and relatives may teach different methods, or share information that does not match your school curriculum. Try not to get frustrated by this. The most important thing is to keep lines of communication open. Share school expectations with parents. Explain how the school approaches the curriculum. Invite parents into your classroom so that they can observe how effectively their child is learning in your classroom.

This leads me onto the last teacher tip for this section.

Teacher Tip

Try to find time at the end of a school day to share something positive about learners with their parents. Make it a target to have a positive conversation with the parents of every pupil at least once a term.

Summary

In this chapter, we have explored:

- motivating your learners by modelling positive approaches to learning and by being a learner yourself

- working with colleagues to share and develop your expertise through developing cross-curricular approaches to learning and teaching

- resourcing your classroom to support your learners including drawing on other adults from the community and using both the indoor and the outdoor environment.

Interpreting a syllabus

5

Introduction

A syllabus tells you what you are expected to teach. There are many forms of syllabus but essentially they provide a list of topics, often called 'learning objectives', showing the content that you are expected to use to plan your lessons. The syllabus may apply at national level. In this case it will be called a 'National Curriculum'. Or it may be a syllabus for international schools in a range of countries. International schools that are part of the Cambridge International family will use the Cambridge Primary Programme to develop a syllabus for their school.

You will see that I have been using the word 'curriculum' interchangeably with 'syllabus'. This is intentional. This book is part of a series which covers all secondary curriculum areas as well as teaching in the primary school. Secondary teachers will be more used to looking at a subject-specific syllabus within a broader curriculum. For primary teachers, the two terms are used interchangeably.

What should I look for in a syllabus?

Broad aims of a syllabus

As well as listing the content that you are expected to teach, many syllabuses also contain a statement of values or expectations about the purpose of teaching a particular subject or possible broader outcomes for learners. For example, the Cambridge Primary programme describes how learners should develop the critical skills needed to respond to the wide range of texts and media that they will meet outside school. It says that learners should develop a holistic understanding of Mathematics which allows them to apply their mathematical knowledge in real-world situations.

When working with a new syllabus, the first thing for a primary teacher to do is to make sure they understand these aims. It is easy to forget the underpinning reasons behind the teaching when we start planning from objectives. It is important that we keep note of the overall aims of our teaching so we can audit our practice occasionally to check we are meeting these aims across all the subjects we teach. In 1949 Ralph Tyler proposed four fundamental questions that we should ask ourselves whenever we design a syllabus from which to teach. These are:

- What educational purposes am I trying to attain?
- What experiences can I provide that are likely to attain these purposes?
- How can I effectively organise these experiences?
- How can I find out if my learners are attaining the aims of the syllabus?

Consider these questions whenever you plan a programme of study. They will help you to think about both the overall aims and the day-to-day experiences of your learners as you plan.

Teacher Tip

Convert the broad aims and purposes of education in your school into learner language and display them on the wall. This allows you and your learners to focus on wider issues of learning. One example might be: 'Learners in my class ask good questions and are good listeners.'

A programme of study

You may be expected to design a scheme of work for your own classroom, or you may be given a scheme of work that has been developed by your colleagues. The scheme of work will give you:

- a long-term overview of all the topics that should be taught during the year
- a medium-term plan broken down at a weekly or half-termly level
- often a weekly plan which suggests the content, and sometimes activities on a lesson-by-lesson basis.

This may seem to take away any autonomy but there is still plenty of work for a teacher to do.

I will use Cambridge Primary Science as an example. At the top level there is a statement that 'An enquiry-based style of teaching and learning is stimulated (by the curriculum) with scientific enquiry objectives integrated throughout to encourage the learning of these skills alongside the scientific concepts'. So, your first task is to make yourself aware and become comfortable with the school's interpretation of 'scientific enquiry'.

Consider Jamaica, where a new Mathematics curriculum has recently been introduced. A teacher in a Jamaican primary school will read that there are five strands to the syllabus: number, measurement, geometry, algebra, and statistics and probability, and that these should be covered cyclically – visiting each strand once a term. The teacher's next task is to look at the long-term plan set out in the scheme of work for each strand, in order to understand how the syllabus is organised.

Finally, you will find the learning objectives that you are expected to teach. For example, in the English National Curriculum one of the learning objectives states that learners should be taught to 'name and locate the world's seven continents and five oceans'. You have an important decision to make. How will you choose to teach your learners the names of the continents and oceans? Of course, you could just tell them and make them memorise the names. But the overall aim states that 'a high-quality Geography education should inspire in pupils a curiosity and fascination about the world'. It is unlikely that just being told information and being tested on it will inspire curiosity and fascination, so a more interesting approach may be expected.

Teacher Tip

Make learning objectives learner-friendly. This helps the learners self-assess at the end of a unit of work. For example, the objective above might be reworded as 'I can find the continents and oceans on a map'.

The next thing to consider in this chapter relates to Tyler's third fundamental question: how can you turn a lesson objective into an effective learning experience?

Structuring and scaffolding learning using a syllabus

Remember to start from the syllabus, then choose an activity you think will best ensure that the learners successfully gain the skills or knowledge you want them to learn. Ideally, think of two or three different ways that you could approach this topic, and then decide which one you think will best meet the needs of the particular group of learners you are working with this year. If you are working with a class with broader educational needs, try to take these into account in your planning.

Teacher Tip

Many teachers write a learning objective on the board at the start of the lesson. Make sure that the learners understand this objective. It is helpful to include a 'process objective' in addition to an objective based on knowledge or skills. For example, you might write, 'Everyone will participate in the group discussion'.

You need to plan the types of questions that you will ask learners in order to support them in their learning. Your focus should be on probing questions. A probing question does not allow for a yes/no response and does not simply test memory. It digs a little deeper and allows you to sense how much deep learning of a subject has taken place. Examples of probing questions in History might be:

• Why do you think that is a true account?
• How did you come to that conclusion?
• What other information do you need?
• Whose perspective are you approaching this from?

Such questions suggest a different approach from simply memorising dates of important events. The use of probing questions will be covered in more detail in Chapter 7 **Assessment for Learning**.

Building assessment into a programme of study

Tyler's final question prompts you to consider how you will know if you have met the aims and objectives of the syllabus. There is often a gap between what we teach and what our pupils learn. It is our job to minimise that gap for as many of our learners as possible. We can only do so if we have an efficient way of assessing the impact of our teaching, and we should consider this in every lesson that we plan. For example, you could:

- use a probing question, as described above
- listen carefully to learners as they discuss a question you have asked them
- listen to how learners describe the way they tackled a problem to the rest of the class.

Make sure that you think about it before the lesson. Also remember to ensure that your choice of assessment methods is balanced across a series of lessons.

And finally, share the way you will be assessing success with learners so that they come to understand what counts as success.

Summary

In this chapter, we have explored:

- the aims which underpin a syllabus, including how we match educational experiences to the educational purposes we are trying to attain

- how to develop a programme of study which includes a long-term plan, a medium-term plan as well as daily plans

- how to structure learning experiences from the programme of study by developing learner-friendly objectives and through probing questions.

Active learning

6

What is active learning?

Active learning is a pedagogical practice that places student learning at its centre. It focuses on *how* students learn, not just on *what* they learn. We as teachers need to encourage students to 'think hard', rather than passively receive information. Active learning encourages students to take responsibility for their learning and supports them in becoming independent and confident learners in school and beyond.

Research shows us that it is not possible to transmit understanding to students by simply telling them what they need to know. Instead, we need to make sure that we challenge students' thinking and support them in building their own understanding. Active learning encourages more complex thought processes, such as evaluating, analysing and synthesising, which foster a greater number of neural connections in the brain. While some students may be able to create their own meaning from information received passively, others will not. Active learning enables all students to build knowledge and understanding in response to the opportunities we provide.

Why adopt an active learning approach?

We can enrich all areas of the curriculum, at all stages, by embedding an active learning approach.

In active learning, we need to think not only about the content but also about the process. It gives students greater involvement and control over their learning. This encourages all students to stay focused on their learning, which will often give them greater enthusiasm for their studies. Active learning is intellectually stimulating and taking this approach encourages a level of academic discussion with our students that we, as teachers, can also enjoy. Healthy discussion means that students are engaging with us as a partner in their learning.

Students will better be able to revise for examinations in the sense that revision really is 're-vision' of the ideas that they already understand.

Active learning develops students' analytical skills, supporting them to be better problem solvers and more effective in their application of knowledge. They will be prepared to deal with challenging and unexpected situations. As a result, students are more confident in continuing to learn once they have left school and are better equipped for the transition to higher education and the workplace.

What are the challenges of incorporating active learning?

When people start thinking about putting active learning into practice, they often make the mistake of thinking more about the activity they want to design than about the learning. The most important thing is to put the student and the learning at the centre of our planning. A task can be quite simple but still get the student to think critically and independently. Sometimes a complicated task does not actually help to develop the student's thinking or understanding at all. We need to consider carefully what we want our students to learn or understand and then shape the task to activate this learning.

Active learning in the primary school

When thinking about active learning in the primary school it is worth watching how the youngest pupils learn. If you visit the kindergarten attached to your school, you will see a great deal of *activity*. This is not aimless play. It is activity, often initiated by the young children, through which they are exploring their world and coming to an understanding of how the world works. Young children will return again and again to the same piece of equipment or the same book. They will enjoy repeating the same activity to check that they get the same result; they will enjoy revisiting their favourite text, looking carefully at the images that accompany the text to see what new discoveries await them.

It is also worth reflecting on how effective these young learners have been. They have learned to communicate, often in more than one language. They have acquired a well-developed sense of how the world works. They will probably be able to ask questions about picture books, will be able to compare sizes of things, and may have a sense of how to get from one place to another. So, self-initiated active learning has been effective for many children before they begin more formal education. This suggests that we should see active learning as an important facet of education in the primary school.

I often ask teachers to think of a good learner whom they teach and then list the learning aptitudes that this learner has. This list often includes many of the learner attributes developed by Cambridge International, listed in the following box and available on the Cambridge International website.

All learners should become:

- confident in working with information and ideas – their own and those of others
- responsible for themselves, responsive to and respectful of others
- reflective as learners, developing their ability to learn
- innovative and equipped for new and future challenges
- engaged intellectually and socially, ready to make a difference.

Planning for active learning

All teachers feel confident in planning for active learning in some areas of the curriculum. It would be strange to plan for a PE lesson which was not active, for example, or a Music lesson. However, it is important that learners engage in learning actively in all areas of the curriculum. Think about an area of the curriculum that you feel most comfortable with, in which you have good subject knowledge and which excites you. It is likely that you plan for active learning whenever you plan a lesson for this curriculum area. Similarly, it would not be unusual for you to be more conservative in your planning for an area in which you feel less certain. I am a Mathematics specialist and feel very comfortable planning for open and creative activities in learning Mathematics. I am married to an English specialist who feels similarly at ease planning activities to develop pupils' literacy skills. When I first started teaching I was very reliant on graded reading schemes and my wife was reliant on Mathematics textbooks. We have learned from each other that active approaches, even in areas we feel less comfortable with, support more effective learning.

I will give you an example. I visited a school to explore developing the creative curriculum with the staff. I sat in the first of a series of lessons exploring the Vikings. The teacher of six- and seven-year-olds had the group of 28 sitting in a circle. They had all visited a dressing-up box she had provided and were dressed as 'Vikings'. She had also changed the role-play area so that it was a Viking hut. She asked the pupils what they knew about Vikings and they gradually worked on their current understanding. She moved on to ask what they wanted to know about the Vikings. The pupils suggested they would like to know more about exactly where the Vikings lived, what food they ate, how they travelled and how long ago they existed. These questions formed the History curriculum for the next few weeks. This approach exemplifies active learning. It starts from the pupils' current understanding and uses their interests and questions as starting points.

I asked the teacher if there were areas where she felt less able to be 'creative' and planned for a more didactic approach. She said that Mathematics was an area that she felt she had to teach more didactically. I offered her Lesson idea 6.1.

☑ LESSON IDEA ONLINE 6.1: A MAGICAL PARTY

This lesson allows learners to develop their understanding of ratio and proportion. It also offers lots of opportunities for measuring and calculation.

The teacher's immediate response was to want to teach the learners about ratio so that they would have the necessary skills to carry out the activity. I pointed out that she hadn't felt the need to do this for the Vikings activity. So, we set the activity up as I describe in Lesson idea 6.1, allowed the learners to work in all-attainment groups and gave them time and space to explore the activity in their own way, as you would expect in active learning.

The teacher was amazed with the range of ways that the learners approached the activity. Some groups took their shoes off and used these to measure their own limbs. They then used this ratio to decide the size of the 'Giant' legs from the big footprint. Other groups used a multiplier – they decided that the magical person was three times bigger and so multiplied all their own measurements by three. Some simply made models that fitted the clothing they had been given. As the groups worked on the activities, our role as teachers was to support the pupils and, through careful questioning, to make sure that they were moving on in their understanding of their own mathematics.

The lesson closed with each group sharing their learning; an important element in any session of active learning.

Designing tasks for active learning

The starting point for all planning should be the curriculum. Do not plan to use a task just because it is an activity you have enjoyed before, or because you have just read about it in a book. Instead, look at the scheme of work and develop active learning approaches that will allow the pupils to learn this particular piece of curriculum. Of course, as you gain experience as a teacher, you will have notebooks full of previous active learning ideas and approaches that you can draw on.

Teacher Tip

Keep a notebook of all the good ideas that you read about or observe. You could organise your notes by curriculum area and by topic so that you can easily find them again. I index all my notes carefully at the back of my notebook.

Remember that active learning is not simply about making sure that learners are active. It is about placing them at the centre of the learning experience. This allows them to construct their own learning, using their previous experience. It is important for learners to have plenty of opportunities to articulate their thinking and their current understanding. It may be helpful to have a series of prompts available as you begin to plan for active learning:

- What do I want the pupils to learn?
- How will the task I have designed help them learn this?
- What prior experience can I expect them to use?
- How does the activity I am planning encourage discussion?

- How does the activity I am planning challenge preconceptions or possible misconceptions?
- What probing questions can I ask to move the pupils' learning forwards?

This list suggests prior knowledge of your own. There is your knowledge of the pupils in your class, and their strengths and areas to develop. You will also have knowledge of some of their prior experience, but there may also be surprises. Pupils will have had lots of experiences that you do not know about.

You need to plan for discussion – this does not just happen by asking learners to discuss things. They are much more likely to have a discussion if they have information to analyse, or points of view to compare, or images to interpret. If you are teaching Science or Mathematics, there may be common misconceptions to take into account. For example, you may be teaching about evaporation. A common misconception is that the sun's rays suck up the water in the puddle. You could design a lesson which could counter this misconception. Similarly, young children may think that the largest parcel in a pile is also the heaviest. This would be another great starting point for an active lesson.

☑ LESSON IDEA ONLINE 6.2: CONCEPT CARTOONS IN SCIENCE

A concept cartoon gives a pictorial representation of commonly held ideas about Science. This lesson idea encourages pupils to discuss their understanding of the weather.

Make sure that learners feel comfortable taking part in discussions. They should feel able to offer their opinions without worrying about being wrong. Develop an ethos of openness and trust in your classroom so that learners are confident that their opinion is valued. This has been described as developing a learning community. You could do this by using drama games at the beginning of sessions, or at the start or the end of the day. Examples of these games are:

- **The trust circle:** One pupil stands in the centre of a circle of six other pupils with their eyes closed. They hold themselves rigid and gradually lean onto one of the other pupils until they are supported by them. The other pupils then gradually support them and move them around the circle.

- **Crossing the circle:** All the pupils sit on chairs arranged in a circle. The teacher makes a statement such as 'Cross the circle if you walked to school.' All the pupils that this applies to cross the circle. The statements can be adapted to relate to the particular theme of a lesson. For example, a lesson on Geography could focus on places that people had visited. The game also works well if there is one chair fewer than the number of pupils. The pupil left standing decides on the next rule for crossing the circle.

The second game point above asks you to think carefully about the probing questions that you might ask to move learning forward. The next section explores this in more depth.

☑ LESSON IDEA ONLINE 6.3: WHAT DO WE KNOW? WHAT DO WE WANT TO KNOW?

This lesson uses rotating flip charts to assess current knowledge about a topic – for example, in History (this technique can be used across the curriculum).

Questioning to encourage active learning

One of the most important changes a teacher can make to move towards active learning is to change the focus of their questioning. As learners, many of us experienced a teaching approach that was characterised by closed questioning as a way of testing our knowledge or memories. One phrase that is often associated with teachers is 'Hands up'. Many of us will also remember how we tried to disguise our lack of knowledge; putting hands half-way up in the hope that we wouldn't get picked, or trying to hide behind our friends.

A shift in practice that you can easily make is to move away from asking learners to put their hands up. Instead, decide who you are going to question and vary your questioning appropriately. This begins to shift questioning to place the learner at the centre.

Try to move towards asking more open questions, to which you do not know the answer. The answers to these questions will give you information about the learner's current understanding and allow you to suggest ways that they might move forward. Examples of probing questions might be:

- Why do you think that was the result?
- What would happen if…?
- What do you think the next step should be?
- How do you know you are correct?
- What strategies did you use to solve that problem?
- What do you need to know to move forward?

Another advantage of probing questions is that you can ask them of any learner and do not have to differentiate your questioning.

Teacher Tip

Write the name of each pupil on a lollipop stick and put them in a jar. When you are asking questions select a stick and ask the pupil whose name is on the stick. This way the pupils know that they could be required to answer any question. And you will have to plan your questioning carefully so that any pupil can respond.

Creating conditions for active learning

I have been lucky enough to work with teachers in over 25 different countries. I often ask them how the classroom that they were taught in as young pupils was organised. It is amazing how alike the responses are. Many describe a classroom arranged in a way similar to those in Figures 6.1 and 6.2.

Figure 6.1: A classroom in England photographed in the early 20th century, arranged in rows.

Figure 6.2: A modern-day classroom in Tanzania, arranged in rows.

The arrangement consists of pupils sitting behind desks, often positioned in rows, all facing the teacher and some kind of board. This may have changed over the years from a blackboard and chalk, to a whiteboard and pens, to a smart board, but the basic arrangement stays the same. Pupils face the teacher who will present them with information. This presents a challenge to us if we are planning for active learning. Remember that active learning places the pupil at the centre. These classroom arrangements clearly place the teacher at the centre.

I was recently working in an international school in Germany. The room had a traditional layout as I have described above, but once the teacher had introduced the lesson he asked the learners to 'Find a space in which you are comfortable working and someone who will support you in your learning for the next part of the lesson'. The pupils worked in pairs or groups of three, self-selecting. Some sat on the floor, others sat on beanbags which were in one corner of the room. Some moved desks together and others just turned chairs round to work with the pupil behind them.

A blog by the American Society for Innovation Design in Education ('Feng Shui for learning') describes how they experimented with different classroom arrangements to suit the learning activity that was taking place. The diagrams in Figure 6.3 show some of the arrangements that they tried out.

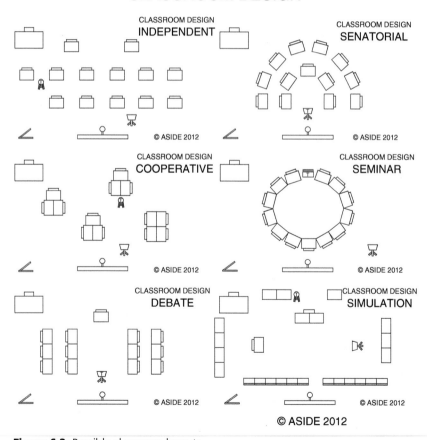

Figure 6.3: Possible classroom layouts.

They suggest that some arrangements were more effective than others but were also certain that rearranging the classroom led to more active learning.

Teacher Tip

Reorganise your classroom on occasions so that the arrangement of desks or tables better supports the type of activity that you are encouraging. How does the layout support active learning, and how does it hinder it?

The document 'Development matters in the Early Years Foundation Stage' (available at the Foundation Years website) from the UK offers another checklist for teachers wishing to create the conditions for active learning in their classroom. This document suggests that teachers who are providing the conditions for active learning make sure that:

- resources which are relevant to learners' interests and background are used
- indoor and outdoor spaces are available in which learners can explore, create and move
- role play is used to support learning
- calm and quiet spaces are available as well as more creative spaces
- there is planned opportunity for playful learning
- if we can develop our classrooms in this way, we can build on the skills of active learning that our pupils developed as young learners.

Summary

In this chapter, we have explored:

- the idea that active learning places the pupil at the centre of learning
- the rationale for using active learning in your classroom
- the learning dispositions of an active learner
- how you can plan for active learning and design tasks that will support active learning
- how to create the classroom conditions for active learning.

7 Assessment for Learning

What is Assessment for Learning?

Assessment for Learning (AfL) is a teaching approach that generates feedback that can be used to improve students' performance. Students become more involved in the learning process and, from this, gain confidence in what they are expected to learn and to what standard. We as teachers gain insights into a student's level of understanding of a particular concept or topic, which helps to inform how we support their progression.

We need to understand the meaning and method of giving purposeful feedback to optimise learning. Feedback can be informal, such as oral comments to help students think through problems, or formal, such as the use of rubrics to help clarify and scaffold learning and assessment objectives.

Why use Assessment for Learning?

By following well-designed approaches to AfL, we can understand better how our students are learning and use this to plan what we will do next with a class or individual students (see Figure 7.1). We can help our students to see what they are aiming for and to understand what they need to do to get there. AfL makes learning visible; it helps students understand more accurately the nature of the material they are learning and themselves as learners. The quality of interactions and feedback between students and teachers becomes critical to the learning process.

45

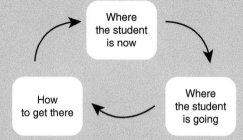

Figure 7.1: How can we use this plan to help our students?

We can use AfL to help our students focus on specific elements of their learning and to take greater responsibility for how they might move forward. AfL creates a valuable connection between assessment and learning activities, as the clarification of objectives will have a direct impact on how we devise teaching and learning strategies. AfL techniques can support students in becoming more confident in what they are learning, reflective in how they are learning, more likely to try out new approaches, and more engaged in what they are being asked to learn.

What are the challenges of incorporating AfL?

The use of AfL does not mean that we need to test students more frequently. It would be easy to just increase the amount of summative assessment and use this formatively as a regular method of helping us decide what to do next in our teaching. We can judge how much learning has taken place through ways other than testing, including, above all, communicating with our students in a variety of ways and getting to know them better as individuals.

Assessment for Learning in the primary school

As a primary school teacher you are at an advantage over your colleagues teaching older learners, as you spend most of the day with your pupils. This should allow you to develop positive relationships with them and get to know their strengths and weaknesses. You will also learn how they can be encouraged to take risks and the areas they are passionate about, as well as those in which they are less interested. So, you are already implementing Assessment for Learning. As the introduction suggested, AfL informs your future planning at an individual and whole-class level and provides immediate feedback to pupils about their current achievements and what they need to do next to progress. There are four strands to AfL in the primary classroom. These are:

- **Sharing learning objectives and success criteria:** This means that learners know what is expected of them in the lesson and understand what the lesson is about.
- **Giving quality feedback:** This is feedback that allows pupils to understand what their next steps in learning should be.
- **Creating a questioning ethos in the classroom:** Teachers ask open and probing questions, and learners develop a questioning approach to learning.
- **Using peer- and self-assessment:** This allows learners to recognise success in their own learning and in their peers' learning.

I will deal with each of these areas in turn in this chapter.

Sharing learning objectives and success criteria

If you do one thing as a result of reading this book, never again start a lesson by asking, 'Now, who can tell me what we learned/covered last time?' The problem is that the teacher's next response may be,

'No – what we learnt is …'. While teachers often split their days up into chunks of subject material and lesson objectives, learners are much more focused on the immediate.

Rather than having learners trying to guess what you want them to say, try starting a lesson with an activity that draws on the learning from the previous lesson and signposts the learning that is about to take place. This will allow you to move on to sharing the learning objectives in a context in which they make sense. As I suggested in Chapter 6 **Active learning**, it is important that the learning objectives are not taken directly from the syllabus but are 'translated' into learner-friendly language.

Next, be explicit about how you will measure success. How will you assess whether or not the pupils have met the learning objective? For example, if your learning objective is something like 'To write an effective factual text', then success criteria might be 'Readers will understand the key facts about the topic'.

Try to avoid 'process' criteria such as 'My writing has an introduction'. This is because a factual text can have an introduction and not be effective in supporting readers to understand key facts, which is the whole point of factual writing. Another possible success criterion might be 'My writing inspires people to find out more about the topic', which is something we would want factual writing to do.

The success criteria can then be revisited at the end of the lesson. Learners can share pieces of writing to assess them. Ask them to evaluate the piece of writing they have been given. Does it summarise key facts in a way that they can understand? Does it inspire them to find out more about the topic? They should discuss this in groups and suggest ways in which the writing meets the success criteria and how it may be improved.

Teacher Tip

Prepare peer-assessments which you can use regularly for this process (see Figure 7.2). This will allow learners to become skilled in assessing against success criteria.

Figure 7.2: Two stars and a wish peer-assessment sheet.

☑ **LESSON IDEA ONLINE 7.1: WRITING A NEWSPAPER REPORT**

This lesson idea illustrates how success criteria can be used when devising a newspaper report.

Giving quality feedback

All teachers have both received and given feedback. We have all experienced having an observer feeding back on a lesson we have just taught. Perhaps you have felt, as I have, that all the positives, usually given at the start of the feedback, pass by in a blur as I wait for the '*but*' or '*however*'. This is exactly how it feels for a learner. How can we avoid this? A starting point is to ask questions. Rather than offering judgement, ask the learner, 'How well do you think you met the success criteria?' The answer to this question will tell you a lot about how much has been understood and how effective the learner is at judging their own progress. In this way feedback is always linked directly to the learning intention and the success criteria.

It is important for feedback to include suggestions for next steps in learning or ways to progress. These comments need to be as specific as possible. Sometimes this will be a particular skill that needs practice. I always remember being told that if I wanted to kick a football as far as I could, I needed to plant my kicking foot alongside the ball rather than behind it, as seemed intuitive. I did this – the ball went further. Instant success. Often, however, feedback is not as instant as this.

An example of poor feedback that you may have heard when you were training to teach is 'You need to develop your presence in the classroom'. This is poor feedback because it doesn't suggest *how* you might make this improvement. It is likely that anyone who needs to improve their classroom presence already knows this, but doesn't know how to improve it. That is why they still appear nervous in front of a class. Much better feedback would be 'Try standing in different parts of the classroom so that you can observe all the learners during the lesson'. A good observer may even create a classroom map showing a teacher where they stood during a lesson. During the next observation, they could aim to develop their (literal) presence, by moving around the classroom more.

Similarly poor feedback would be 'You need to try to present your write-ups more neatly'. It would be much better to show a learner what you expect. Break down feedback into smaller success criteria and get the learner to focus on one thing at a time.

Carol Dweck, a professor of psychology at Stanford University in the USA, has coined the term 'growth mindset' and this connects to our discussion about feedback. She suggests that some learners (and their teachers) believe in a fixed minsdset, that we are born with abilities and traits which we cannot alter. In some ways, our success, or lack of it, is preordained. Those who believe in growth mindsets, however, believe that we can all grow and develop through engaging in challenging and motivating activity which we will stick at with resilience. As a teacher, a growth mindset allows me to believe that all learners have the possibility to grow if I plan appropriately and I am skilled at giving feedback. Feedback to support the development of a growth mindset will focus on using questions such as:

- How can you improve on that result?
- What did you do when became stuck on that problem?
- What strategies did you use to solve that problem?
- What do you need to learn next to move forward?

Teacher Tip

Try to use questions which will develop a growth mindset. Avoid praising using phrases like 'It was very clever of you to see that' or 'Well done – you are the first to finish'.

Creating a questioning ethos in the classroom

In Chapter 6 **Active learning** you read how important it is to create a classroom in which learners are not afraid to ask questions and take risks. This does not just happen, though. You need to teach your learners how to ask good questions and be open about their thinking without worrying about 'being wrong'.

There are several fairly simple techniques that you can use to develop this classroom ethos.

Talk partners: Assign learners a partner called a 'talk partner'. This should be someone whom they trust and will be open with. These talk partners should be used regularly for very short bursts of discussion. This could be for the 'question of the day' (see Teacher Tip below), to discuss success criteria or to try to support a learner who has made an error. Once the idea of talk partners has become embedded in your classroom, you can move away from having fixed talk partners to allocating partners at random, so that over a year every learner gets to experience the thoughts and ideas of every other learner.

Teacher Tip

Start each day with a question of the day which requires creative or lateral thinking. An example might be, 'How many uses can you think of for a paper clip?' (This is sometimes called divergent thinking.)

Think/Pair/Four/Share: This is a development of talk partners. I have often used the technique for creating a set of classroom rules but it can be used for almost any discussion. First, to take my example, I would ask every pupil to list, individually, five rules that they would expect everyone to follow in the classroom. Then I would ask them to discuss their rules with their talk partner. They should refine the ten rules that they bring together into a set of five rules that they can agree on. The final step is to create a group of four and repeat the process exactly, sharing their rules and agreeing on five rules that all four members of the group think are important.

A simpler version of this strategy just asks pupils to share their ideas with the whole class after talking as a pair.

Graffiti learning: Learners work in groups. I usually put my learners into all-attainment groups to make sure that learners who are less confident with language hear vocabulary modelled by their peers, and more confident learners have to articulate their thinking, which consolidates their learning. Whenever you set a group-work task, give each group a large sheet of flip chart paper to work on and a pen each. They record their thinking or ideas on the piece of flip chart nearest them as they move towards a solution. In this way, everyone's thinking is visible – in fact, 'copying' is encouraged.

☑ **LESSON IDEA ONLINE 7.2: GUESS MY NUMBER/GUESS MY SHAPE**

This lesson uses 'Guess my number' and 'Guess my shape' games to develop learners' ability in asking useful questions.

Using peer- and self-assessment

You will have realised by now that peer- and self-assessment are central to developing effective AfL approaches in your classroom. AfL is about using the results of your assessments to support learners in moving forward. It is even more powerful if learners are able to assess themselves effectively and so understand what they need to do in order to progress. If you develop learners who are effective self- and peer-assessors, you should have a group of learners who are:

- engaged and motivated
- able to give and receive quality feedback
- able to support their own learning through engaging with the learning process
- able to interpret success criteria and assess against them effectively.

Your learners will become skilled at assessing if you build self-assessment and peer-assessment into your everyday practice. This means that learners will get to practise assessing. You may want to use paired discussions at the ends of lessons to evaluate the learning against the success criteria you have agreed, or you may want to provide learners with structured success criteria against which they can assess their own work. You should move learners away from asking closed questions, or assessing against closed criteria. Instead, encourage them to ask evaluative questions such as:

- What aspects of the activity were easy? Which were more challenging?
- When did you get stuck? How did you move forward?
- What do you still need more help with?
- What have you learnt that you didn't already know?
- How would you adapt this activity if you had to teach it?

As you develop your AfL classroom, you may choose to ask your learners to keep learning journals. I find these invaluable in telling me what learning is going on and how effective my teaching is. These learning journals can form the basis of an ongoing, written conversation between you and the learners. In several cases, I also invite parents to comment in these learning journals. You can use the prompts above to support the learners in writing about their learning at the end of a day, or at the end of a unit of work.

One final, less time-consuming strategy is the use of 'traffic lights' cards on the desk. These are a set of three cards – one red, one amber and one green. Red symbolises 'I'm stuck', amber 'I'm finding this difficult' and green 'Everything is fine'.

These can be used by individuals, either during the lesson or at the end, to give you instant feedback on how they have felt.

Teacher Tip

Ask learners to place traffic light cards on their desk and to change them during the lesson depending on their progress. Emphasise that you would expect to see 'red' on occasions as we all need to be stuck if we are challenging ourselves. Similarly 'amber' should signal an opportunity for learners to get support from their peers.

Summary

The key facets of AfL are sharing learning objectives and success criteria, giving quality feedback, creating a questioning classroom and providing opportunities for peer- and self-assessment. In this chapter, we have explored:

- how quality feedback should aim to develop a growth mindset in the learners

- how to teach learners to become effective questioners through appropriate activities

- ways of building peer-assessment and self-assessment opportunities into your day-to-day classroom practice.

Metacognition

8

What is metacognition?

Metacognition describes the processes involved when students plan, monitor, evaluate and make changes to their own learning behaviours. These processes help students to think about their own learning more explicitly and ensure that they are able to meet a learning goal that they have identified themselves or that we, as teachers, have set.

Metacognitive learners recognise what they find easy or difficult. They understand the demands of a particular learning task and are able to identify different approaches they could use to tackle a problem. Metacognitive learners are also able to make adjustments to their learning as they monitor their progress towards a particular learning goal.

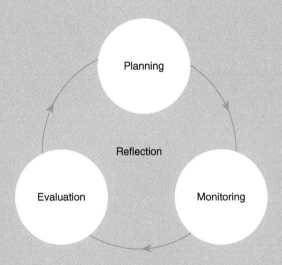

Figure 8.1: A helpful way to think about the phases involved in metacognition.

During the *planning* phase, students think about the explicit learning goal we have set and what we are asking them to do. As teachers, we need to make clear to students what success looks like in any given task before they embark on it. Students build on their prior knowledge, reflect on strategies they have used before and consider how they will approach the new task.

As students put their plan into action, they are constantly *monitoring* the progress they are making towards their learning goal. If the strategies they had decided to use are not working, they may decide to try something different.

Once they have completed the task, students determine how successful the strategy they used was in helping them to achieve their learning goal. During this *evaluation* phase, students think about what went well and what didn't go as well to help them decide what they could do differently next time. They may also think about what other types of problems they could solve using the same strategy.

Reflection is a fundamental part of the plan–monitor–evaluate process and there are various ways in which we can support our students to reflect on their learning process. In order to apply a metacognitive approach, students need access to a set of strategies that they can use and a classroom environment that encourages them to explore and develop their metacognitive skills.

Why teach metacognitive skills?

Research evidence suggests that the use of metacognitive skills plays an important role in successful learning. Metacognitive practices help students to monitor their own progress and take control of their learning. Metacognitive learners think about and learn from their mistakes and modify their learning strategies accordingly. Students who use metacognitive techniques find it improves their academic achievement across subjects, as it helps them transfer what they have learnt from one context to another context, or from a previous task to a new task.

What are the challenges of developing students' metacognitive skills?

For metacognition to be commonplace in the classroom, we need to encourage students to take time to think about and learn from their mistakes. Many students are afraid to make mistakes, meaning that they are less likely to take risks, explore new ways of thinking or tackle unfamiliar problems. We as teachers are instrumental in shaping the culture of learning in a classroom. For metacognitive practices to thrive, students need to feel confident enough to make mistakes, to discuss their mistakes and ultimately to view them as valuable, and often necessary, learning opportunities.

Metacognition in the primary school

There are clear links between the discussion above and Chapter 7 **Assessment for Learning**. AfL techniques include ensuring that pupils are clear about what they are learning and understand success criteria so that they can tell when they are learning effectively. Perhaps one way of understanding the different foci of the two chapters is that AfL is a teacher-led strategy. It is for the teacher to assess pupils' understanding so that they can plan for future learning to take place. Metacognition is a learner-centred notion. A metacognitive child in the primary school is able to plan for their own learning, monitor their own progress and evaluate how successful they have been. In other words, AfL can take place without learners engaging in metacognition. Learners can be metacognitive without AfL strategies being implemented. But learning will be most successful in classrooms where both AfL and metacognition are present.

The planning–monitor–evaluate cycle allows teachers and learners to take a holistic view to learning rather than separating learning off into subject discipline chunks. It also allows teachers to develop strategies that they can use across all subjects.

In Chapter 5 **Interpreting a syllabus** and Chapter 7 **Assessment for Learning** I discussed the importance of sharing learning objectives with learners and ensuring that they understand what these objectives mean. This is vital if we are expecting learners to plan for their own learning. It is also a starting point in developing a classroom that encourages self-regulated learning. But a classroom that focuses on development needs much more than this. Self-regulating, metacognitive learners can:

- understand the possibilities for learning
- activate their prior knowledge in this area
- monitor their learning against success criteria they understand
- reflect on their learning process.

The rest of the chapter will explore each of these areas in turn.

Understanding learning possibilities

You will see that I have replaced 'learning objectives' with 'learning possibilities' in this chapter. This is because there is a tension to be aware of when thinking about learning objectives and metacognition.

I will illustrate this with an example. I was visiting a school whose national curriculum had placed great emphasis on sharing lesson objectives with pupils at the beginning of the lesson. In fact, it was expected practice for objectives to be written on the board and copied down by pupils at the beginning of the lesson. This school did not follow this practice, for good educational reasons which I will discuss later. While I was observing a class, I overheard this conversation between a nine-year-old pupil and a government inspector:

Inspector: What do you think the learning objectives are for this lesson?

Pupil: Something about fractions.

Inspector: But exactly what will you be learning about fractions?

Pupil: Well, I don't know yet. I will tell you at the end of the lesson.

At the end of the lesson the nine-year-old pupil was able to tell the inspector exactly what they had learnt about fractions that they did not know before the lesson started.

If we are not careful, presenting narrow learning objectives at the *beginning* of a lesson can narrow the possibilities rather than open up possibilities for learning. For example, the objectives for the lesson above could have been written narrowly as:

'Know equivalent fractions for ½ and ¼.'

However, there were several pupils in the class who already knew equivalent fractions for ½, ¼ and other fractions. By the end of the lesson there were several who still did not know equivalent fractions for ¼, but were developing an understanding of equivalence. Perhaps a better objective would say:

'Develop our understanding of what makes fractions equivalent.'

This is much more open and allows for all learners to make progress. Wording objectives in this way also meets the well-articulated concerns of our nine-year-old pupil above.

Teacher Tip

Develop learning objectives that are open enough for all pupils to observe progress in a lesson. Objectives should open up possibilities rather than close them down.

Activating prior knowledge

First of all, our pupils need to be clear about the possibilities for learning. Next, they need to be able to access any prior knowledge that will be useful for them in progressing in learning. All pupils will always have some relevant prior knowledge. Lesson idea 8.1 illustrates how this process can be modelled.

LESSON IDEA ONLINE 8.1: MULTIPLICATION FACTS
This lesson idea shows how an activity exploring multiplication facts can be used to develop and encourage metacognition. The lesson models the importance of activating prior knowledge to develop new knowledge.

Lesson idea 8.1 directly challenges learners' preconceptions that the teacher is responsible for deciding how a task should be carried out, and how learning should be activated. It expects learners to take responsibility for their own learning and challenges them to draw on their own prior knowledge to decide for themselves how they can move forward.

It is tempting for teachers to always show learners how to start an activity. However, if we always model the learning process, we do not allow metacognition to develop. Learners will come to rely on teachers to show them how to do things, rather than begin to think for themselves. You will be able to tell when you are becoming successful in supporting learners in activating their prior knowledge as they will stop asking you how they should start an activity, or asking your permission to try a certain approach, and will, instead, tell you why they have chosen a particular approach.

Teacher Tip

At the end of a lesson, share with the whole class all the different ways in which pupils chose to approach an activity. This models different strategies so that all your pupils can develop new approaches. It also makes it clear that you expect them to develop their own strategies.

Another way to support pupils in activating prior knowledge is to open a lesson with an activity which allows them to draw on their prior knowledge. For example, the lesson I discussed about equivalent fractions in 'Understanding learning possibilities' could have started with an activity asking pairs or small groups to draw or write down as many representations of 'a half' as they could (Figure 8.2).

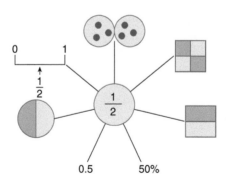

Figure 8.2: Representations of $\frac{1}{2}$.

Another example of activating and drawing on pupils' prior knowledge effectively is Lesson idea 7.1 in the previous chapter. This encouraged pupils to use their prior knowledge of recent events and their knowledge of what engages them in a newspaper article.

At this stage, we have learners who:

- are clear about the possibilities for learning
- have drawn on their prior knowledge to make sense of the activity for themselves
- have planned how they will engage with the activity.

The next stage is for learners to be able to monitor their progress.

Monitoring learning

Whenever a teacher asks me to observe them in developing their learners' metacognitive skills, I carry out a simple experiment. I time how much of the lesson is taken up with teacher talk and how much with pupil talk. They are usually amazed by the imbalance. Teachers often talk for much longer than they think!

Teacher Tip

Involve the pupils in carrying out an experiment in your classroom. Give two pupils stopwatches, one to time you and one to time the pupils. Alternatively, ask a colleague to do this. After you have been supporting pupils in developing metacognitive skills, repeat the experiment.

I start with this example as an important part of monitoring learning is through developing what Robin Alexander has called 'dialogic teaching' in the classroom. Dialogic talk takes place when teachers and learners both make extended and significant contributions to a conversation about the learning that is taking place. The vocabulary that learners develop through such dialogic talk allows them to better monitor their learning. In Chapter 3 **The nature of the subject**, you read how Vygotsky thought all learning came about through social interaction. Here we see this theory in action. There are several simple strategies you can use to encourage learners to make more extended contributions to classroom discussions.

- Build thinking time into a question – do not expect or allow immediate responses.

- Ask for pair discussion to take place first before asking for contributions.
- Move questioning around pupils by asking, 'Can anyone extend that idea?'
- Allow pupils to rehearse answers – ask them to share something that you heard them say during the lesson.
- Prompt longer contributions by saying, 'Could you tell me a little more about that?' or 'I'm not sure I quite understand; can you expand on that a little?'

Encourage pupils to use whole-class discussions throughout the activity to monitor learning, rather than simply responding at the end of a lesson. This can be done through a process of 'checking-in' using mini plenaries to allow pupils or groups of pupils to share the progress they are making.

It is vital that the process of monitoring learning includes seeing mistakes as a positive and important part of learning. People at the forefront of their disciplines, particularly in the scientific disciplines, spend most of their lives making mistakes, spotting these mistakes and correcting them to move forward. Piagetian theory, which I introduced in Chapter 3 **The nature of the subject**, is based on the assumption that we will notice something that jars with our current understanding of the world. We will then learn to accommodate this new understanding.

It is worth spending time at the end of an activity asking pupils to tell you about the points at which they became stuck and what they did to move forward. This helps develop metacognitive processing and acknowledges that the ethos of the classroom is to expect mistakes. The list below is taken from an article in *Mathematics Teaching 250* by Sarah Punshon called 'We're stuck'. She interviewed scientists about how they responded when they became stuck.

- Explain it out loud to someone else.
- Try to break it down into smaller steps.
- Say what I know already.
- Try a simpler version.
- Doodle.
- Double-check all my answers so far.
- Draw a picture of the problem.
- Think quietly for a bit longer.
- Write down what I know and what I don't know.

- Check I understood the question.
- Ask someone else for help.
- Stare out of the window for a moment and just think.
- Write it out again, really neat.
- Draw a picture, with different colours for the different things.
- Have a guess: it'll probably be wrong, but working out why it's wrong can be useful.

Teacher Tip

Develop a poster labelled 'What to do when you're stuck' by listing all the strategies that learners use. Whenever a learner tells you that they are stuck, simply point to the poster to make it clear it is their job to find ways to move forward.

☑ LESSON IDEA ONLINE 8.2: MAKING HISTORY

This lesson idea uses drama to emphasise the importance of 'not knowing' to move forward. It also expects learners to share and draw on prior knowledge and experience.

The final issue to consider is how we can develop the skills of reflection in our learners so that they see reflection as a natural part of learning.

Reflecting on learning

I briefly mentioned learning journals at the end of Chapter 7 **Assessment for Learning** as a useful strategy to support learners in assessing themselves. Reflection is more than monitoring how successful we have been. By reflecting we think back over the whole learning process and think through strategies that were successful, strategies that were less successful and strategies we could apply in other areas. Pupils who become reflective are able to think about learning in general and about themselves as learners, both in general and of particular subjects. In fact the most skilled reflective learners will notice how they may learn slightly differently in different subjects.

I think that asking pupils to keep learning journals is the most effective way to develop reflective learners. Assign a time at the end of each day for pupils to keep their journals. You can encourage creativity and support them to use whatever form of journal suits them best. This could include mind maps, blogs, wikis, graphics – this is an area in which creativity should be encouraged.

Use prompts to support learners' thinking. Display prompts such as these on the classroom wall:

- What did I find easy to learn today? Why?
- What was most challenging for me today? Why?
- When did I get stuck? How did I move forward?
- What do I know now that I didn't know when I came to school?
- What do I want to learn about as a result of my learning today?
- Who helped me to learn? What did they do?
- What skills do I need to develop to learn better?

▣ LESSON IDEA ONLINE 8.3: LETTERS TO FUTURE LEARNERS

This lesson idea uses letter writing to support pupils in reflecting on their learning by writing to future pupils.

Recognising a self-regulating classroom

Teachers need to be metacognitive too. We need to see ourselves as students as well as supporting those in our classrooms to become effective learners. So the first thing I expect to see in a 'self-regulating' classroom is a teacher who sees themselves as a student and expects to be continuously learning, both in terms of developing as a teacher and learning new subject knowledge.

A self-regulating classroom has:

- pupils who can articulate the possibilities for learning at the beginning of a session and can reflect on their learning both during and at the end of a session
- pupils who offer extended answers without prompting; evenly balanced time for teacher talk and pupil talk
- pupils (and a teacher) who see making mistakes and getting stuck as important parts of the learning process
- evidence of the teacher's own learning shared with the pupils.

Teacher Tip

Use the points above to observe your own classroom. If your pupils are becoming self-regulating, there will be time to do this. Share your observations with the pupils so that they come to understand the behaviours you expect to see.

Summary

The focus of this chapter is how you can encourage and develop metacognition in your classroom to create more self-regulated learners who take responsibility for their own learning and have well-developed metacognitive skills. We have explored:

- how pupils need to have a clear understanding of your aims for the lesson so they think carefully about how to approach the activity

- how you can teach pupils effective methods to plan for, monitor and evaluate their own learning effectively

- how to develop a dialogic ethos in your classroom to encourage pupils to continuously monitor their learning.

9 | Language awareness

What is language awareness?

For many students, English is an additional language. It might be their second or perhaps their third language. Depending on the school context, students might be learning all or just some of their subjects through English.

For all students, regardless of whether they are learning through their first language or an additional language, language is a vehicle for learning. It is through language that students access the learning intentions of the lesson and communicate their ideas. It is our responsibility as teachers to ensure that language doesn't present a barrier to learning.

One way to achieve this is to support our colleagues in becoming more language-aware. Language awareness is sensitivity to, and an understanding of, the language demands of our subject and the role these demands play in learning. A language-aware teacher plans strategies and scaffolds the appropriate support to help students overcome these language demands.

Why is it important for teachers of other subjects to be language-aware?

Many teachers are surprised when they receive a piece of written work that suggests a student who has no difficulties in everyday communication has had problems understanding the lesson. Issues arise when teachers assume that students who have attained a high degree of fluency and accuracy in everyday social English therefore have a corresponding level of academic language proficiency. Whether English is a student's first language or an additional language, students need time and the appropriate support to become proficient in academic language. This is the language that they are mostly exposed to in school and will be required to reproduce themselves. It will also scaffold their ability to access higher order thinking skills and improve levels of attainment.

What are the challenges of language awareness?

Many teachers of non-language subjects worry that there is no time to factor language support into their lessons, or that language is something they know little about. Some teachers may think that language support is not their role. However, we need to work with these teachers to create inclusive classrooms where all students can access the curriculum and where barriers to learning are reduced as much as possible. An increased awareness of the language needs of students aims to reduce any obstacles that learning through an additional language might present.

This doesn't mean that all teachers need to know the names of grammatical structures or need to be able to use the appropriate linguistic labels. What it does mean is that we all need to understand the challenges our students face, including their language level, and plan some strategies to help them overcome these challenges. These strategies do not need to take a lot of additional time and should eventually become integral to our process of planning, teaching and reflecting on our practice. We may need to support other teachers so that they are clear about the vocabulary and language that is specific to their subject, and how to teach, reinforce and develop it.

Language awareness in the primary school

Many of the subjects that you will teach involve learners becoming familiar with technical vocabulary. This vocabulary will vary from subject to subject and can place high demands on young learners throughout the day. We must also remember that the language of instruction, English, may not be the first language of the teacher or the pupil.

It is important that when you plan a lesson, you focus on just three or four key pieces of technical vocabulary. It is worth writing these key words on the board at the beginning of each lesson as a reminder to yourself and to the learners to focus on these words. As you progress through a unit of work, you can gradually build up a bank of key words that are important to the area you are studying.

Teacher Tip

Build subject-specific glossaries that you can refer to as you progress through a unit of work. Do this over a series of lessons so you do not introduce too much new vocabulary at once.

Where possible, link the key words to images or pictures to make the key words accessible to all pupils whatever their level of English language competence. These key words can also be displayed as a 'word wall' (Figure 9.1).

☑ LESSON IDEA ONLINE 9.1: SCIENCE – HEALTHY EATING

This lesson uses images and a word bank to develop pupils' understanding of key vocabulary around healthy eating.

Approaches to learning and teaching Primary

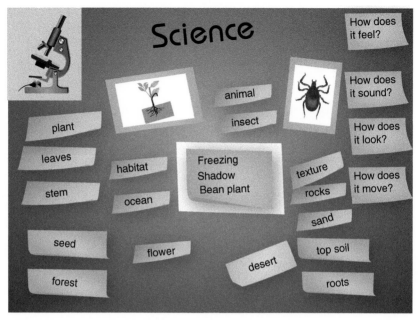

Figure 9.1: A Science word wall.

The key principles that underpin developing language awareness in the primary classroom are:

- Introduce a few key words at a time and explain them carefully.
- Introduce the words when they are needed to move learning forward.
- Avoid teaching a lot of new vocabulary at the beginning of a lesson.
- Use an appropriate context accessible to the learners to explain the key words.
- Repetition is important – keep referring to the key words.
- Link the words to pictures or actions.
- Encourage learners to develop their own glossaries.
- Make the learning of language active and enjoyable as with all other learning.

☑ LESSON IDEA ONLINE 9.2: MATHEMATICS – AREA AND VOLUME

This lesson idea illustrates a way to support learners to develop their own glossary when exploring geometry.

What are the challenges of language awareness for primary teachers?

Teachers in international primary schools are often much more language-aware than their colleagues in state schools who do not teach through the medium of English. It is very likely that the pupils they teach will come from homes in which different languages are spoken. Similarly, and positively, the pupils will be language-aware. They will understand that different people speak a range of languages. While it is important to celebrate such language diversity, it is also vital that the learning is not negatively impacted by the use of a second language to teach the content.

This will raise concerns for you which include:

- your own knowledge of English and the necessary technical vocabulary
- the wide range of English competence and confidence in your pupils
- developing resources which support language development as well as subject understanding
- developing assessment tools which assess pupils' understanding rather than their competence in English.

These concerns can be met positively by developing a language-rich environment.

Creating a language-rich environment

Non-native English speakers can have an advantage when teaching in a multilingual classroom. They have an awareness of the importance of language and will often take more care when explaining key terms, not taking understanding of these terms for granted. Key strategies to make sure that 'teacher talk' is accessible to all learners include:

- keeping your language simple
- keeping your sentences short

- pronouncing key words carefully and slowly pointing to the posters of flash cards you have prepared
- clarifying meaning using visuals, by acting key words out or by using realia
- using signs around the classroom for important everyday words.

A language-rich environment includes supporting learners to develop their listening and reading skills. These require understanding rather than production of English speaking and writing, which make different demands in terms of the 'performance' of English.

When you plan a lesson or a series of lessons, think carefully about how you will support listening and reading. As suggested above, make sure any key vocabulary is introduced before setting any reading or listening tasks. If you are reading aloud, you can point to key vocabulary that is displayed. If learners need to access vocabulary when reading worksheets or instructions, support them using images.

I often use the following as an example when I am working with teachers.

Initially I ask the teachers to sit silently and write the following question on the board. I ask them to try to answer the question and tell them I will give them two minutes.

Utfor overslagrakning och svara med heltal.

a. 3,56. 7,2   b. 10,6. 3.3   c. 5,9. 9.7

Unless there happens to be a Swedish speaker in the group, there follows two minutes of embarrassed silence. I then allow the teachers to talk to each other to work on the question. This relieves the tension and there are some attempts to carry out calculations.

Then I put up the graphic shown in Figure 9.2.

Figure 9.2: Language awareness activity (*Talking Maths, Talking Languages*. The Association of Teachers of Mathematics).

This is often sufficient for them to make progress but finally I add the key vocabulary:

Ar mellan: is between

Narmast: nearest

This allows all the participants to proceed. This simple activity emphasises how important it is to allow pupils to discuss the questions being asked in their home language, the importance of supporting language with graphics and how vital it is to clarify the meanings of key words.

Teacher Tip

When preparing worksheets for learners, include graphics where possible. List the key words and their meanings at the top of the worksheet.

You also need to think carefully when you are planning for learners to either speak or write in English. Think about the language demands of the particular activity so that you can plan appropriate strategies to support the learners to use English to perform the activity. Table 9.1 illustrates possible language demands and the appropriate language support.

Language demand	Language support
Technical vocabulary required by the task	Flash cards or displays available illustrating this vocabulary
Key phrases or sentences required	Provide writing frame or sentence starters
Key words for the feedback or assessment section of the lesson	Model the use of this key vocabulary during the lesson when working with learners. Encourage learners to work in groups where those less confident in English will hear their peers using the key vocabulary

Table 9.1: Examples of language support.

If you reflect on previous chapters, you will see how the strategies to support active learning, AfL and metacognition also support learners in their language development.

Working in a multilingual environment

I was working with a PhD student who, although very skilled in English, spoke Arabic as his first language. At one tutorial, we were discussing how hard he was finding it to write one particular chapter. I asked him to tell me the key points he wanted to get over in Arabic. 'But, you don't speak Arabic!' he said. 'No – but I am a good listener in Arabic', I said. For the next 20 minutes he talked to me, in Arabic, and I listened, nodding and smiling even though I could not understand a word. At the end of the 20 minutes he said, 'Now I know what I need to write.' Through describing his key ideas and concepts in Arabic, he had come to an understanding of what he needed to write in English. He needed to think in his first language before he could write in a second language.

So, creating a language-rich environment does not mean that the only language on view or in evidence should be English. It is important to use and develop the first language abilities of your pupils, as their progress in developing their English language skills is closely linked to their proficiency in their first language (L1). It is often easier to understand concepts in your first language and important to be able to discuss the meanings of concepts and ideas in L1. You can encourage the use of L1 in your classroom by developing bilingual and multilingual displays (Figure 9.3).

Figure 9.3: A multilingual display.

Other techniques to use L1 to support learners develop their English skills are:

- using bilingual subject-specific dictionaries with older learners
- encouraging discussion in L1 and then reporting back in English

- using bilingual flash cards for key vocabulary
- taking notes in L1 but writing reports in English
- annotating English texts or labelling diagrams using L1
- writing first drafts in L1 and then revising drafts in English.

This also means that learners' first languages must be valued in the classroom. You can create a language-rich environment by using the range of languages available to develop all learners' linguistic diversity.

Teacher Tip

Find out how many different languages are spoken by the pupils in your class. Ask pupils to teach the whole class how to count to 20 in their first language. Find out which languages belong to the same language family and which words are shared.

Through this approach your own language skills will develop and you will come to love the sound of many different languages being spoken simultaneously. Indeed, you may find it strange when you experience an environment in which only English is spoken.

Summary

The focus of this chapter is to support you in developing a language-rich classroom in order to encourage English language development in a multilingual environment. We have explored:

- how to focus on key vocabulary introduced carefully when it is necessary to move learning forward

- how you can develop a word wall of pupil glossaries to support language development

- the importance of planning carefully so that you have strategies in place to support all the language demands of the tasks pupils are expected to carry out.

10 | Inclusive education

What is inclusive education?

Individual differences among students will always exist. Our challenge as teachers is to see these differences as opportunities to enrich and make learning accessible for all, and not as problems. Inclusion is an effort to make sure all students receive whatever specially designed instruction and support they need to succeed as learners.

An inclusive teacher welcomes all students and finds ways to accept and accommodate each individual. An inclusive teacher identifies existing barriers that limit access to learning, then finds solutions and strategies to remove or reduce those barriers. Some barriers to inclusion are visible; others are hidden or difficult to recognise.

Barriers to inclusion might be the lack of educational resources available for teachers or an inflexible curriculum that does not take into account the learning differences that exist among all students, across all ages. We also need to encourage students to understand each other's barriers, or this itself may become a barrier to learning.

Students may experience challenges because of any one or a combination of the following:

- behavioural and social skill difficulties
- communication or language disabilities
- concentration difficulties
- conflict in the home or caused by political situations or national emergency
- executive functions, such as difficulties in understanding, planning and organising
- hearing impairments, acquired congenitally or through illness or injury
- literacy and language difficulties
- numeracy difficulties
- physical or neurological impairments, which may or may not be visible
- visual impairments, ranging from mild to severe.

We should be careful, however, not to label a student and create further barriers in so doing, particularly if we ourselves are not qualified to make a diagnosis. Each student is unique but it is our management of their learning environment that will decide the extent of the barrier and the need for it to be a factor. We need to be aware of a student's readiness to learn and their readiness for school.

Why is inclusive education important?

Teachers need to find ways to welcome all students and organise their teaching so that each one gets a learning experience that makes engagement and success possible. We should create a good match between what we teach and how we teach it, and what the student needs and is capable of. We need not only to ensure access but also to make sure that each student receives the support and individual attention that result in meaningful learning.

What are the challenges of an inclusive classroom?

Some students may have unexpected barriers. Those who consistently do well in class may not perform well in exams; or those who are strong at writing may be weaker when speaking. Those who are considered the brightest students may also have barriers to learning. Some students may be working extra hard to compensate for barriers they prefer to keep hidden; some students may suddenly reveal limitations in their ability to learn using the techniques they have been taught. We need to be aware of all corners of our classroom, be open, and put ourselves in our students' shoes.

Inclusion in the primary school

Primary teachers have an advantage over secondary teachers when it comes to developing an inclusive classroom. You spend most of the day with the pupils in your care. This means that you feel responsible for all areas of intellectual and emotional development. You are also acutely aware of the importance of developing positive relationships, and understand the connection between positive relationships and effective teaching and learning.

A young disabled woman called Maresa MacKeith (2012) has written eloquently about her vision of an inclusive education system. She writes:

> My vision is that we create a system of learning that prioritises our relationships with each other rather than how we achieve in competition with each other. In that way, we could learn about each other's needs which we could find ways of meeting. I think that within a generation of having a learning system without competition we could have a world where people were valued for what they can give. Those who most need care would be seen as an opportunity for others to develop relationships and through this understand the commonality of vulnerability. (p. 76)

This powerful plea for celebrating and embracing difference resonates with a multicultural approach to teaching. If you teach in an international school, you are probably already aware of the importance of taking a multicultural approach. Such an approach would:

- recognise and value the range of cultural backgrounds that exist in the classroom, drawing on them in the curriculum
- draw on the wide range of pupils' experience to support learning and teaching
- develop pupils' understanding of cultures other than their own
- ensure there is no bias in teaching materials
- develop positive attitudes to all cultures through the curriculum.

A multicultural approach challenges the idea of stereotyping. One activity that I have used with teachers illustrates the idea of difference within a culture very well. I sometimes work with teachers from a predominantly white Christian background who are teaching in culturally diverse schools. These teachers are keen to understand and empathise with the diverse backgrounds of their pupils.

I start by asking about the range of pupils in their classrooms. The list they come up with is often linked to beliefs and might be something like Sikh, Hindu, Muslim, Jewish or Buddhist. I then ask what characteristics they are interested in. Another list takes shape, often including things such as diet, patterns of worship and dress. We create a grid and spend time thinking about what knowledge there is in the group about these characteristics. The group will usually manage to complete a grid allocating certain characteristics to the faith groups. They may write, 'Hindus are vegetarians' or 'Jewish people don't work on a Saturday or eat pork'.

I then add 'Christian' to the list and ask what characteristics we might write down. The first response is often, 'Oh, but all Christians are different'. We use this as a starting point for discussion around the importance of understanding the nature of beliefs so that we do not inadvertently make a pupil feel uncomfortable, balanced with not making assumptions that groups are 'all the same'. The important point is to make sure we talk to our pupils and their families/carers in order to understand them better.

Teacher Tip

Use circle time regularly to listen to everyone's views about important issues. This is particularly important if world events are of concern to a specific group of learners.

☑ LESSON IDEA ONLINE 10.1: CIRCLE TIME

This lesson idea introduces learners to the ethos of circle time.

Creating an inclusive classroom

Another measure of inclusion in a primary school is the extent to which the school is welcoming to newcomers. At the time of writing, many schools are receiving pupils from families who have been forced to relocate. It is important to work with pupils on creating a welcoming environment for all. You may train pupils to take on a peer-mentoring role for newcomers to the classroom (see, for example, the Mentor and Befriending Foundation's 'Peer Mentoring in Schools', available online, which shows the positive impact of peer mentoring on both behaviour and attainment).

Creating classroom buddies offers similar support to pupils. Some classrooms create 'listening posts'. This is a defined space in the playground or in the classroom where a 'buddy' or a 'peer mentor' will sit at break times in case anyone wants a conversation about problems they are facing. It is important that peer mentors or buddies are trained by you before they take on these roles. Particular skills you will need to develop are:

- how to lead by example
- how to be honest in responses to questions
- how to listen well
- how to give positive feedback
- how to be patient
- knowing when to ask for support.

Teacher Tip

A good way to develop positive self-esteem among all your learners is 'Learner of the day'. At the start of each day, select a new child to be the 'Learner of the day'. At the end of the day, ask the rest of the class to think of something positive they have noticed about this learner during the day. Record them on the 'Learner of the day' board.

⊡ LESSON IDEA ONLINE 10.2: CREATING A WELCOMING CLASSROOM
This lesson idea suggests a way of using Drama to develop a welcoming classroom.

A key part of developing an inclusive classroom is the involvement of parents and carers. They are part of your inclusive classroom too, and should feel involved in all aspects. Work in partnership to celebrate successes and solve problems that relate to the children they care for.

Some parents may find it difficult to start conversations about their worries, particularly around issues of inclusion. Some parents may themselves have felt excluded at school and it is particularly important to reach out to them. Try to develop an ethos of what Carl Rogers has called 'unconditional positive regard'. This means accepting and supporting people, no matter what they do. This is sometimes interpreted as focus on the action that has caused a problem rather than seeing an individual as a problem.

Try to be an active listener to parents. Allow them to articulate their concerns without being defensive or judgemental. Once they have finished speaking, try to summarise their concerns and ask how they would like the problem to be solved. You can then work together to come up with a solution. Avoid having a predetermined solution before you meet the parent. There are four phases to a structured conversation:

1   Explore: Give the parent time to outline the issue. Listen actively and paraphrase what you think they have told you, to check your understanding.
2   Focus: Identify priorities together. What do you both see as the key issues?
3   Plan: Agree what you want to happen as a result of the conversation, and the next steps you will both take. Set targets if appropriate.
4   Review: Agree when you will meet to review progress.

Teacher Tip

Have a quiet space where you can meet parents/carers to discuss their concerns. This space should not have tables which might act as a barrier. Also make sure that you are available for informal conversations at the beginning and the end of the day. Initiate conversations with parents at these times.

An inclusive classroom is not a place where there are no rules. It is a place, however, in which all pupils will feel as though they were included in deciding on the rules. Chapter 7 **Assessment for Learning** offered suggestions for different ways to group pupils and the think/pair/four/share strategy can be used to develop a shared set of 'golden rules' for the classroom.

Meeting specific needs

There are many labels that can be attached to pupils to denote their specific learning needs. As suggested in the introduction to this chapter and emphasised by Maresa MacKeith, these should not be seen as 'special'. This label would suggest that anyone who does *not* have a specific learning need is somehow more 'normal' than other pupils. Maybe it is better to consider all pupils as having specific needs at specific times. So, while always wanting to see beyond any label, this section explores strategies that can be used to support pupils who have had a particular label attached.

Emotional and behavioural difficulties

A learner with emotional and behavioural difficulties will often have a heightened emotional response to day-to-day events in the classroom. This behaviour may take the form of disruptive, anti-social or aggressive behaviour and it may well impact on other learners in the classroom. It may also lead to poor relationships with their peers, hyperactivity or attention and concentration problems.

I have suggested in earlier chapters that open-ended problem-solving tasks can help pupils to take more responsibility for their learning. These sort of tasks can exacerbate behavioural difficulties if pupils are uncertain what is expected or how to start them. They may avoid starting these tasks in case they do not meet your expectations. For these learners it may be helpful to provide a tighter structure with time-specific targets being set.

Try to maintain consistent routines in the classroom so that learners know what is coming next. Avoid surprises. It is also important to model processes and summarise learning and expectations regularly. Learners often respond well to being given responsibility – perhaps by standing in front of the class to demonstrate. This also allows you to model positive behaviour.

Aim to avoid interrogational questioning as learners may feel humiliated and this can be a cause of inappropriate behaviour. Finally, make sure that you offer all learners a challenge. Avoid offering low-level tasks in the hope that this will keep them busy. It is more likely to lead to boredom and inappropriate behaviour.

Autism

The National Autistic Society in the UK describes autism as a lifelong developmental disability. Autism is seen as a 'spectrum disorder'. Although people with autism share three main areas of difficulty, the condition affects each person in a different way. Indeed, it is often said: 'If you have met one person with autism, you have met one person with autism.' The three main areas of difficulty are:

- social communication
- social interaction
- social imagination.

Autism is one of the 'hidden disabilities, and parents of children who have been identified as being on the autistic spectrum often report that teachers of their child in earlier years saw them as simply 'naughty'. This shows how important it is to work hard to understand the cause of inappropriate behaviour through conversations with the pupil and with their parents or carers.

As a teacher, it is important to be careful when you set up pair work or group work. This can be problematic for learners on the autistic spectrum. This does not mean you should not use pair or group work. On the contrary, this will help learners to develop positive relationships, but, as mentioned above, make sure you stick to routines. For example, you may ask pupils always to sit in the same place when they come to the carpet or gather round the front. Make sure that pupils have a personal space that they can always go back to and where they feel secure.

Transitions should be planned carefully as these are other stress points for pupils on the autistic spectrum. Be clear about how movement between activities will be calm and orderly. Simply sending pupils back to their desks after a demonstration can feel overwhelming. If a pupil becomes overwhelmed by the noise, then allow them to go to their quiet, calm space for a while. Sudden noises can be very stressful for some pupils. Try to be understanding rather than judgemental.

Using familiar equipment and manipulatives is also important. Novelty has little appeal to many learners on the autistic spectrum. Also be aware that these learners may take everything you say literally – so be careful with your use of metaphor. Taking time to observe how the learners are responding to your explanation and instructions will be helpful for your future planning.

Finally, allowing pupils to 'fiddle' with an object can help their concentration. People with autism report that having something to occupy their fingers or listening to music actually shuts out other distractions.

Recent films and stories in the media seem to suggest that many people on the autistic spectrum can calculate huge numbers in their heads or have photographic memories. Unfortunately such stories give the false impression that all children with autism have these special skills. Most people on the spectrum do not have any special talents for Mathematics. However, some children on the autistic spectrum may exhibit keen interests in particular subjects, and so may know a great deal about very specific areas.

The UK-based National Autistic Society, the Autism Society of India and the Singapore-based Autism Association have links to autism helplines and charities around the world, and can be used as a starting place to search for the appropriate charity for the country in which you work.

Dyspraxia

Pupils on the autistic spectrum often exhibit signs of dyspraxia too. In fact, dyspraxia is thought to affect up to 10% of the population. Dyspraxia is a developmental delay to the way in which the brain processes information to help organise movement. In other words, pupils with dyspraxia can often appear clumsy. Dyspraxia can also lead to difficulties in perception, language and thought.

As with learners described above, avoid giving a long series of instructions for a task as this will be confusing. Make sure you break down your instructions step by step. Giving thinking time is also helpful.

It is also helpful if you do not change the arrangements of desks too much or leave materials around the room that could be hazards. This is also helpful for learners with visual impairments.

Dyslexia

Dyslexia is characterised by difficulties in processing word sounds and by weaknesses in short-term verbal memory. Its effects may be seen in spoken language as well as written language. The current evidence suggests that these difficulties arise from inefficiencies in language processing areas in the left hemisphere of the brain which, in turn, appear to be linked to genetic differences.

Don't ask a child with dyslexia to read questions aloud unless you are sure they will be comfortable doing this. By checking individual needs, you will know what specific support your dyslexic pupils may need. It may be that coloured filters will support them in reading text, or printing on a particular colour of paper. The use of highlighters to pick out key words is an important skill for all learners and will support dyslexic pupils across all subjects.

Providing visualisation activities will help dyslexic pupils – indeed they may excel in this area and be able to support other children in becoming more skilled at visualisation.

Dyslexia International is a not-for-profit charity which provides training for teachers around the world to help them better support learners with dyslexia.

Dyscalculia

Dyscalculia describes people who have specific difficulties in carrying out calculations. This may be a result of damage to specific regions of the brain, or may occur developmentally, as a genetically linked learning disability which affects a person's ability to understand, remember or manipulate numbers or number facts. The term often refers specifically to the inability to perform arithmetic operations, but it is also seen as leading to a specific difficulty in conceptualising numbers as abstract concepts, or 'number sense'.

Ways that you can support learners with dyscalculia include providing a wide range of concrete manipulatives to help understanding to develop before moving into the abstract concepts. This will also assist in providing learners with strategies to visualise. When working on problem-solving or word problems, try to provide opportunities to use real-life situations or items to assist with visualisation.

It can also help to provide opportunities to use 'pictures, words or graphs' to help with understanding. Make sure you promote a 'can do' attitude as much as possible; praise and a positive outlook can start to overcome the fear of Mathematics that learners with dyscalculia may have developed.

A blog entitled 'Dyscalculia Blog', based in Spain, has links to a range of resources in France, Germany, Spain and Hungary.

Summary

The focus of this chapter is how you can develop an inclusive classroom. The strategies suggested for supporting learners with specific learning needs can support all learners. The chapter has explored:

- how to create a classroom that is welcoming to all learners and their families

- the importance of finding out about specific needs through observation and discussion with learners and their families

- the importance of avoiding stereotyping and treating all learners as individuals rather than as representatives of particular groups.

11 | Teaching with digital technologies

What are digital technologies?

Digital technologies enable our students to access a wealth of up-to-date digital resources, collaborate locally and globally, curate existing material and create new material. They include electronic devices and tools that manage and manipulate information and data.

Why use digital technologies in the classroom?

When used successfully, digital technologies have the potential to transform teaching and learning. The effective use of technology in the classroom encourages active learning, knowledge construction, inquiry and exploration among students. It should enhance an existing task or provide opportunities to do things that could not be done without it. It can also enhance the role of assessment, providing new ways for students to demonstrate evidence of learning.

New technologies are redefining relationships and enabling new opportunities. But there are also risks, so we should encourage our students to be knowledgeable about and responsible in their use of technology. Integrating technology into our teaching helps prepare students for a future rooted in an increasingly digitised world.

What are the challenges of using digital technologies?

The key to ensuring that technology is used effectively is to remember that it is simply a resource, and not an end in itself. As with the use of all resources, the key is not to start with the resource itself, but to start with what you want the student to learn. We need to think carefully about why and how to use technologies as well as evaluating their efficiency and effectiveness.

If students are asked to use digital technologies as part of their homework, it is important that all students are able to access the relevant technology outside school. A school needs to think about a response to any 'digital divide', because if technology is 'adding value', then all students need to be able to benefit. Some schools choose to make resources available to borrow or use in school, or even loan devices to students.

Safety for students and teachers is a key challenge for schools and it is important to consider issues such as the prevention of cyber-bullying, the hacking of personal information, access to illegal or banned materials and distractions from learning. As technology changes, schools and teachers need to adapt and implement policies and rules.

One of the greatest pitfalls is for a teacher to feel that they are not skilled technologists, and therefore not to try. Creative things can be done with simple technology, and a highly effective teacher who knows very little about technology can often achieve much more than a less effective teacher who is a technology expert. Knowing how to use technology is not the same as knowing how to teach with it.

Digital technologies in the primary school

The Educational Endowment Foundation (EEF), which draws on large-scale studies in education to calculate the value of particular innovations in the classroom, suggests that the use of digital technologies can increase attainment by four months for a moderate cost (their report is available on the Foundation's website). They add the caveat that digital technology should be used to supplement, rather than replace, your teaching. In other words, you should continue to plan carefully for your own teaching and draw on digital technologies when they can supplement your teaching effectively. The digital technologies do not change the way in which children learn but they can impact on the way in which you will interact with your pupils, or the range of representations available to pupils to develop their understanding.

In fact, the pupils in your class will already be interacting with digital technologies in their own time. They will be playing games, engaging with social media and using the internet to track down information. In fact they will be much more in touch with latest developments than you.

Teacher Tip

Spend time with pupils exploring their use of digital technologies. Use them as experts and take their advice on how best this technology can be used in the classroom. This also allows you to point out possible safety issues with the pupils' use of digital technologies – particularly social media.

The challenge for you as a teacher is to make sure that your use of digital technology allows for more effective learning to take place rather than simply replacing your current teaching practices.

Approaches to learning and teaching Primary

Findings of the EEF *Report on the Impact of Digital Technology on Learning* (Higgins, Xiao and Katsipataki, 2012) that are useful for primary teachers include:

- Using technology in pairs or small groups of learners is more effective than individual use. So, avoid software which simply offers individual practice or rote learning.
- Digital technology is most useful when used for short, focused interventions.
- The use of technology to provide tutorial support for lower attaining learners has proved effective in allowing them to 'catch up' with their peers.
- Digital technology has proved particularly effective in raising attainment in Mathematics and Science.
- Technology is most effective when teachers have undergone a full day's training to support the introduction of new technology. It is also effective where there is an ongoing programme of professional development in inquiry-based learning.

Their overall conclusion is that technology can be a catalyst for change but cannot make the change in teaching and learning approaches on its own. There are several questions that you can ask before you introduce a new piece of technology:

1 Will it support learners in working together more effectively? How will it make the learning process more productive?
2 Will it allow learners to access knowledge in new ways?
3 Does the technology offer alternative models of knowledge that cannot be accessed in other ways?
4 How will the technology support collaborative learning?
5 Does the technology offer feedback to learners or will you need to plan new ways to support the learning through formative feedback?

As a way of thinking these issues through, it may be worth reflecting on the last time you introduced a new piece of digital technology into the classroom. There are four possibilities for this implementation. You may have used the technology as follows:

- As a direct **substitute** for what you were already doing. There was no change to your teaching pedagogy.
- To **augment** what you were already doing. In this case the resource for learning may have changed but classroom practice did not.

- To **modify** the activity of learning task that you have used previously.
- To **redefine** the teaching and learning process.

Reflect on how you have introduced new technology. If you are not modifying or redefining the learning in the classroom, are you making the best use of the new technology?

I recently visited an international school and spent time in the classrooms across the whole of the primary school including kindergarten. In this school, every child had access to a tablet. I will offer a brief cameo of a lesson to illustrate how such technology can be used.

The teacher gathered the whole class around them to introduce the focus of the lesson. Pupils did not bring any equipment with them. The focus in this section of the lesson was the teacher. As the teacher outlined the new ideas, pupils wrote notes or drew images on a flip chart. At the end of the introductory session, the completed flip chart was displayed along with several others from previous lessons in the week. Several pupils took photographs of this flip chart on their tablet to refer to at home.

The pupils were then assigned differentiated tasks. These were all available on the tablet. The pupils accessed them via the school intranet. They could choose whether to work individually, in pairs, or in small groups. They could also find a space in which they felt comfortable to carry out the tasks. There were beanbags as well as tables and chairs available.

Several of the tasks involved using the tablets for research. The school firewall ensured that pupils could research safely.

At the end of the lesson, groups of learners had prepared presentations on their tablets which they could show directly on the interactive whiteboard through the use of a dedicated piece of software.

This is clearly an example of digital technology having redefined the learning and teaching process.

Teacher Tip

Use an application such as *splashtop* or *chromecast* to allow your pupils to mirror the tablet they are using on the interactive whiteboard in your class. Encourage pupils to use their tablets to report on their learning.

☑ **LESSON IDEA ONLINE 11.1: 'THE FLIPPED CLASSROOM'**
This lesson idea uses 'the flipped classroom' to offer an alternative to your traditional classroom teaching.

Digital technologies fall into two groups: those that we use as a teaching tool and those which are primarily technologies for learners to use to enhance their learning.

Digital technologies as a teaching tool

The interactive whiteboard

One of the most obvious changes in classrooms over the last 20 years has been the introduction of interactive whiteboards (IWB) into classrooms. The first interactive whiteboard was introduced in 1991 and now the only places that I will now see 'blackboards' and chalk are in less developed countries that do not have the economic resources or reliable access to electricity which such technology requires.

This does not mean that the pedagogy I observe has been revolutionised in the same way. I visit many classrooms and the teaching style is still similar to that which predated the IWB. The slide presentation has replaced the notes written on the blackboard, but little else has changed. The focus of the beginning of the lesson is still teacher exposition – the learners' role at this point is to listen. The learners will then be set tasks either on worksheets or from a workbook which they complete.

If that last point sounded rather gloomy, I must add that I have often seen the IWB used with great effect. I have seen learners motivated and excited by games which develop their mathematics skills such as countdown, which can be downloaded for free. I have seen teachers using clips from films or documentaries to great effect to support creative writing; using the full IWB screen to browse art galleries or finding clips of musicians performing to inspire are all approaches which would not have been possible 15 years ago.

It is important that you think how best the IWB can be used to support active learning, AfL, and developing a language-aware and inclusive classroom. One way in which you can begin to do this is to plan for pupil engagement with the interactive whiteboard. Make sure that learners have access to the IWB, either to add to your notes or to develop presentations of their own.

Teacher Tip

Even though it is very tempting to stick to a presentation once you have planned it, make sure that you can be flexible. Explore the use of alternative presentation software such as *prezi* which allows you to develop more flexible presentations.

Visualisers

Another piece of technological hardware which is appearing in more classrooms is a visualiser. These have only been available since 2010, and at first they were mainly used as a replacement for the old overhead projector. Rather than placing a slide on the projector, a teacher would place a worksheet on the visualiser which would then project this onto a screen. In many ways it is appropriate to see a visualiser as a modern overhead projector. The main advantage is that you can place anything underneath the camera of a visualiser and it will be projected onto a screen. You do not have to prepare an acetate slide. I have seen visualisers used to enhance teaching and learning in the following ways:

1   Sharing learners' work in order to support peer-assessment. Placing a diagram or a piece of written work from a learner on the visualiser

allows all the class to see it clearly. You can use a strategy such as 'two stars and a wish' (see Figure 7.2) to support peer-assessment.

2   Modelling the use of manipulatives such as Cuisenaire rods or place value counters. Pupils do not have to crowd round a desk at the front of the classroom to try to see what you are doing. They can also model how they have used manipulatives to solve a problem.

3   Sharing a Science experiment with the whole class. Again, this removes the need for all the pupils to gather around a single desk.

4   Some visualisers come with powerful magnifying devices attached. These are particularly useful for Science investigation.

☑ LESSON IDEA ONLINE 11.2: DEVELOPING A BLOG

Your pupils may already be reading blogs online. This lesson idea supports their creative or factual writing skills by developing their own blog.

Digital technologies for learners

Learners can use digital technologies in many ways: they may use digital cameras to take images which will support research projects they are engaged in; they may use their smartphones to record interviews with family members as a part of a History project; they can use spreadsheets to record and represent data; they can use presentation software to share the results of their investigations with the whole class or the whole of the school. However, each of the possibilities comes with a health warning (Table 11.1).

Use of technology	Warning
Blended and virtual learning	This cannot replace teacher subject knowledge. Plan carefully to ensure that learners can understand content and that there is a place for teacher input.

Use of technology	Warning
Game-based learning	Ensure that games are supporting learning that is in the curriculum. Avoid using games simply to fill time when other activities are completed.
Accessing digital content	Make sure that you monitor this. A lot of digital content available online is inaccurate. Encourage learners to select trustworthy sources, or to check information by using several different sources.
Active participation in online communities	Ensure that all your pupils understand about safety and engaging in online communities.
Using technology to collect and curate	Make sure that there is a 'quality control' process and that the learners are not simply putting everything up that they find on a topic. This is a good opportunity for peer-assessment.

Table 11.1: Using technology carefully.

Staying safe online

It is important that you teach the learners in your class how to stay safe online. There are many useful websites that you can use, including Childnet International. They use the acronym SMART to help learners remember safe practice when using the internet. This stands for:

S: **Safe** – keep safe by never giving out personal information online. This includes your address, your email, any phone numbers or any passwords.

M: **Meet** – never agree to meet someone that you have met online. If someone suggests meeting in person, tell your parents or your teacher straight away.

A: **Accept** – never accept images or other files that are sent as attachments to emails or text messages. These could contain viruses or unpleasant images.

11

R: **Reliable** – always check information that you read on the net with a reliable source. Just because something is on a social media site or Wikipedia does not mean it is true.

T: **Tell** – always tell your parents or your teacher if anything online makes you feel worried.

Teacher Tip

Make sure that you educate your pupils about online safety (for example, using resources such as those available from the Internet Matters website). Many online resources also have materials that you can share with parents/carers.

▣ LESSON IDEA ONLINE 11.3: SHAPES EVERYWHERE

This lesson idea uses digital technologies to support learners' understanding of shape. It also uses very old-fashioned technology!

Keep up to date

The hardest part of utilising new technologies in the classroom is the speed of change. New apps for tablets and new pieces of educational software are released every day, and it is easy to feel overwhelmed by the pace of progress. Make use of your learners: they are often the ones that hear about new ways of using IT first. Make time to listen to how the pupils are using technology. Ask them what is new in social media and which sites they are using most. Use their expertise to explore ways of bringing the latest ideas into your classroom.

Use social media yourself to support your professional development. There are many useful meetings using Twitter which take place, and you will quickly find the people to follow who can keep you up to date with developments.

Summary

The focus of this chapter is the impact that the use of digital technologies can have on learning and teaching in the primary classroom. The chapter has explored:

- how digital technology is best used as a collaborative resource

- the importance of careful planning to make sure digital technology enhances the learning experience

- the importance of spending time familiarising yourself with new technologies before you introduce them into your classroom

- how to ensure you have made your pupils aware of safety issues.

12 Global thinking

What is global thinking?

Global thinking is about learning how to live in a complex world as an active and engaged citizen. It is about considering the bigger picture and appreciating the nature and depth of our shared humanity.

When we encourage global thinking in students we help them recognise, examine and express their own and others' perspectives. We need to scaffold students' thinking to enable them to engage on cognitive, social and emotional levels, and construct their understanding of the world to be able to participate fully in its future.

We as teachers can help students develop routines and habits of mind to enable them to move beyond the familiar, discern that which is of local and global significance, make comparisons, take a cultural perspective and challenge stereotypes. We can encourage them to learn about contexts and traditions, and provide opportunities for them to reflect on their own and others' viewpoints.

Why adopt a global thinking approach?

Global thinking is particularly relevant in an interconnected, digitised world where ideas, opinions and trends are rapidly and relentlessly circulated. Students learn to pause and evaluate. They study why a topic is important on a personal, local and global scale, and they will be motivated to understand the world and their significance in it. Students gain a deeper understanding of why different viewpoints and ideas are held across the world.

Global thinking is something we can nurture both within and across disciplines. We can invite students to learn how to use different lenses from each discipline to see and interpret the world. They also learn how best to apply and communicate key concepts within and across disciplines. We can help our students select the appropriate media and technology to communicate and create their own personal synthesis of the information they have gathered.

Global thinking enables students to become more rounded individuals who perceive themselves as actors in a global context and who value diversity. It encourages them to become more aware, curious and interested in learning about the world and how it works. It helps students to challenge assumptions and stereotypes, to be better informed and more respectful. Global thinking takes the focus beyond exams and grades, or even checklists of skills and attributes. It develops students who are more ready to compete in the global marketplace and more able to participate effectively in an interconnected world.

What are the challenges of incorporating global thinking?

The pressures of an already full curriculum, the need to meet national and local standards, and the demands of exam preparation may make it seem challenging to find time to incorporate global thinking into lessons and programmes of study. A whole-school approach may be required for global thinking to be incorporated in subject plans for teaching and learning.

We need to give all students the opportunity to find their voice and participate actively and confidently, regardless of their background and world experiences, when exploring issues of global significance. We need to design suitable activities that are clear, ongoing and varying. Students need to be able to connect with materials, and extend and challenge their thinking. We also need to devise and use new forms of assessment that incorporate flexible and cooperative thinking.

Global thinking in the primary school

Some primary teachers have suggested to me that the earlier stages of education should focus on local issues rather than global issues. They believe that young learners are not able to grapple with the wider global dimension and the complex debates surrounding globalisation and internationalism. However, the Cambridge Primary Review Trust highlighted how important it is for primary schools to have a global perspective, in their report 'Primary Education for Global Learning and Sustainability' (February 2016). They suggested that issues such as migration and climate change have an everyday impact on all children's lives and that the use of digital technology (see Chapter 11 **Teaching with digital technologies**) means that children of all ages have immediate access to knowledge of these global events.

The 2015 United Nations sustainable development goals called for 'all students [to] acquire the knowledge and skills needed to promote sustainable development through education for ... global citizenship'. This reinforces the argument that learners in the primary school should be supported to become global citizens. But what might a global citizen look like, and how do they differ from a citizen of the country in which they learn?

Oxfam (2015) describe a global citizen as someone who:

- is aware of the wider world and has a sense of their own role as a global citizen
- respects and values diversity
- has an understanding of how the world works
- is passionately committed to social justice
- participates in the community at a range of levels, from the local to the global
- works with others to make the world a more equitable and sustainable place
- takes responsibility for their actions.

The first of these bullets emphasises how important it is that our pupils have an awareness of the wider world, so let us explore this in more detail.

Awareness of the wider world

As I have stated before, teachers in international schools are at an advantage in this debate. It is likely that you work with a diverse set of children. It is also likely that the pupils in your class speak a range of languages and have family members around the world. They may even have travelled themselves. Pupils in international schools in which I have worked and many of the beginning teachers I work with around the world describe themselves as 'third culture kids'. This term refers to children who are raised in a culture other than that of their parents.

I was recently at a wedding between a bride who was an Iranian Kurd with refugee status in the UK, and a groom, a second-generation Englishman whose grandparents had fled the Ukraine during the Second World War. I met a family at the wedding consisting of a mother who is a recent immigrant from Poland, a father who is a monolingual Englishman and two bilingual children (aged eight and two) who speak only Polish to their mother and only English to their father. The children have already spent a lot of time with their grandmother and cousins in Poland. They will naturally have a much greater awareness of the wider world than young people who have only experienced a monolingual, homogeneous home life and classroom.

So, the place to start developing an awareness of the wider world is to find out about the lives and life histories of the pupils in your classroom. It is very likely that this will increase your understanding of the wider world too. One quick way to do this and to stimulate conversation and discussion is to buy a large world map for your classroom. It would be even better to find a parent or other member of your school community who is artistic and who can create a mural for your classroom wall.

Give each member of your class a series of sticky notes in different colours. Ask them to place these on the map to show:

- the place I was born
- places that I have family
- places that I visit.

Teacher Tip

Involve your pupils' families/carers in the activity above. Invite them to visit your classroom early one afternoon and ask your pupils to describe the activity to their families/carers. The visitors can engage in the same activity. This will allow them to make new connections for themselves.

☑ **LESSON IDEA ONLINE 12.1: AN INTERNATIONAL HOUR**
This lesson idea draws on parents and community expertise to develop learners' awareness of the wider world through the eyes of their peers.

These activities will stimulate much discussion. They will also show you which countries the pupils in your class have not experienced. This gives you a good starting point for researching global issues that the class do not have personal experience of. Small groups of pupils can take responsibility for researching a different country, and they can present their findings to the rest of the class (and the families/carers if possible).

Coming to a better understanding of the wider world

The previous section described how you can draw on your pupils' current understandings and backgrounds to support their developing awareness of the global dimension. We also discussed how pupils can research those areas that they are not currently aware of to explore wider global issues.

School twinning

A twinning project is an ideal way to raise your pupils' awareness of wider global issues. This is particularly effective as the pupils develop this understanding through communication with peers. The first thing you will need to do is to find a partner. The British Council website has a large database of schools willing to participate in twinning projects. You can decide on the country that you would like to twin with and then find a school.

Most schools use Skype or another conferencing tool to make contact, and schools with experience in twinning all stress how important it is to keep in regular contact. They have also found it useful when both twinned schools work on a shared project such as designing the car of the future.

The most important advice is to plan carefully and have realistic expectations and timeframes for developing the twinning. It is also important that pupils in both schools plan for the first 'face-to-face' meeting. Email questionnaires and introductions have an important role to play here.

Teacher Tip

You may be able to draw on community contacts that you already have to set up a twinning project. Explore the links that families/carers of your pupils have to see if there are connections that you can take advantage of.

Global issues

There are many global issues that you can use across the curriculum in the primary school. The global distribution of water can be explored in Geography. This can be linked to the water cycle in Science and Mathematics can be used to explore the data about access to clean water.

Climate change and global warming is another area that can be explored through the Science curriculum. There are clear links to be made with literacy here if you wish to write letters or present research reports on how these issues are affecting children around the world.

The internet is a source of information about the use of child labour around the world and this can be explored through Drama.

Teacher Tip

Go to the website of Global Dimension, an educational charity that promotes global learning, to find many case studies of how the global dimension has been used to develop lessons across the whole primary curriculum.

The book *If the World Were a Village* (David J. Smith and Shelagh Armstrong, 2004) presents data which allows for rich discussions around global issues. It models data by imagining the world as a village of 100 people and describing the village using the data. For example:

> In the village, 61 people are from Asia; 13 are from Africa; 12 are from Europe; 8 are from South America, Central America and the Caribbean; 5 are from Canada and the United States; 1 is from Oceania.

Data includes languages spoken around the world, world religions and access to electricity and clean water. Such statistics are always changing, so a useful class project would be to research and update the information.

☑ **LESSON IDEA ONLINE 12.2:** *IF THE WORLD WERE A VILLAGE*
This lesson idea uses the book *If the World Were a Village* to develop understanding of global issues in a Mathematics lesson.

Working with others to make the world a more equitable place

It is tempting to avoid trying to deal with global issues through a concern for upsetting young children. As a young teacher I remember working on autobiographies with a group of eight-year-olds. As we were engaging in the work, I became aware that one of the pupils had arrived in the country alone, sent to safety by their parents. I asked my headteacher whether I should ask the pupil to work on an alternative activity. The refugee charity workers and the school management convinced me that it was vital not to avoid difficult life histories. In fact it was an important part of the healing process to engage in normal classroom activity. It is likely that in your career you will work with pupils whose families face danger from war and other threats. It is important that the classroom becomes a safe place for the worries and concerns of our pupils to be discussed.

As a teacher, it is important to become skilled at making space for discussion. Use the circle-time techniques from Chapter 11 **Teaching with digital technologies** to respond to your pupils' concerns. Use resources from the internet to respond to contemporary issues – there are articles relating to the art that is being created in refugee camps, for example. You can also draw on literature written from a wide range of global perspectives.

Teacher Tip

Once a month base your circle time on current news reports. Bring a range of newspapers into school and let small groups of children spend some time reading them. Move into a circle-time activity to discuss the issues raised.

Philosophy for Children and global issues

Philosophy for Children, or P4C, is an approach which, when introduced carefully, can allow children to discuss and think through issues which may normally be considered too difficult for them. The aim of P4C is to develop learners' critical thinking skills through an enquiry approach which allows them to seek understanding rather than simply gaining knowledge, and to support learners in reflecting on these new understandings to move towards taking action.

A P4C session will usually start with a stimulus which will provoke questions in the learners. Small groups of learners then write down the questions that they wish to ask as a result of the stimulus. The class then comes together and selects an open question to discuss as a whole class. The circle-time techniques we have already discussed are very helpful here.

P4C and other techniques to support discussion can be very powerful in getting learners to think as global citizens. It can also lead them to take particular lines of action in response to their discussions. P4C emphasises the importance of creating a collaborative environment in which all points of view are heard and taken seriously. This kind of environment is at the centre of developing global citizens.

Developing global thinking in the primary classroom is not simple. But nothing is simple in your classroom. If you engage in the types of activities described, you will not be seen by the learners as providing answers, rather you will be seen as someone who encourages them to think carefully about issues in order to come to their own answers. And, to return to the opening of this book, that is what an enquiry approach is all about.

Issues of sustainability

Issues of sustainability can make the link between local and global issues effectively. Figure 12.1 represents the extent of global access to water 'if the world were a village of 100 people'.

This can be used to make the link to waste and to saving resources where possible. Many primary schools are in areas where it is necessary to save water. There will be a range of sustainability issues in the area where you teach. Any issue in the country where you work is also an issue in your classroom. You can spend time discussing issues of waste with your learners. For example:

- Travel to school – do too many staff and pupils travel to school by car? Is there an alternative?
- The use of paper – is a lot of paper wasted? Photocopiable resources use both paper and power to produce. What alternatives could be used?
- Could power be saved by more effective use of electricity for lighting or air conditioning?

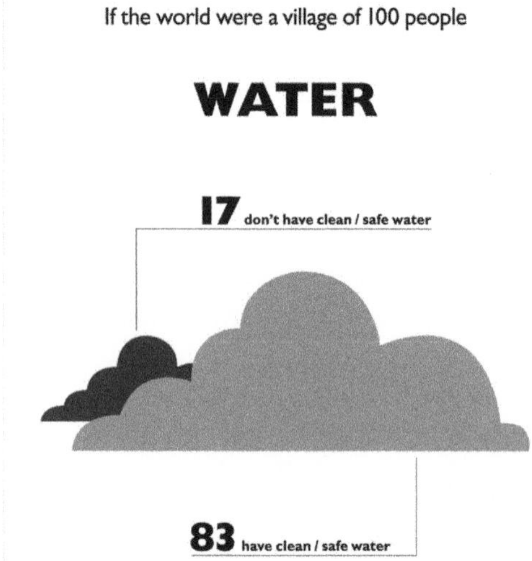

If the world were a village of 100 people

WATER

17 don't have clean / safe water

83 have clean / safe water

Figure 12.1: Access to water if the world were a village of 100 people.

This discussion will lead to many fruitful areas for research. Learners can research the situation themselves and report back to the rest of the school. They may even be able to suggest changes to the management of the school. I have known of schools where some of the money that has been saved through more careful use of resources has been used to pay for a special event planned by the pupils themselves.

A project such as this shows the slogan 'Think Global, Act Local' in action at a classroom level.

Summary

The focus of this chapter is how global thinking can be explored in the primary classroom. We have explored:

- the importance of discussing global issues in the primary classroom

- how to use the experience and backgrounds of your pupils and their families/carers to develop their understanding of the world

- the advantages of twinning with a school in another part of the world to help learners to develop global understanding

- the importance of dealing with sensitive issues carefully – your pupils may well be affected by them.

Reflective practice

13

Dr Paul Beedle, Head of Professional Development
Qualifications, Cambridge International

'As a teacher you are always learning'

It is easy to say this, isn't it? Is it true? Are you bound to learn just by being a teacher?

You can learn every day from the experience of working with your students, collaborating with your colleagues and playing your part in the life of your school. You can learn also by being receptive to new ideas and approaches, and by applying and evaluating these in practice in your own context.

To be more precise, let us say that as a teacher:

- you **should** always be learning
  to develop your expertise throughout your career for your own fulfilment as a member of the teaching profession and to be as effective as possible in the classroom.
- you **can** always be learning
  if you approach the teaching experience with an open mind, ready to learn and knowing how to reflect on what you are doing in order to improve.

You want your professional development activities to be as relevant as possible to what you do and who you are, and to help change the quality of your teaching and your students' learning – for the better, in terms of outcomes, and for good, in terms of lasting effect. You want to feel that 'it all makes sense' and that you are actively following a path that works for you personally, professionally and career-wise.

So professional learning is about making the most of opportunities and your working environment, bearing in mind who you are, what you are like and how you want to improve. But simply experiencing – thinking about and responding to situations, and absorbing ideas and information – is not necessarily learning. It is through reflection that you can make the most of your experience to deepen and extend your professional skills and understanding.

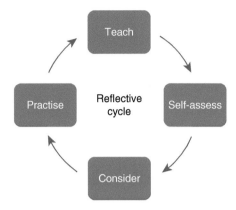

Figure 13.1

In this chapter, we will focus on three *essentials* of reflective practice, explaining in principle and in practice how you can support your own continuing professional development:

1 **Focusing** on what you want to learn about and why.
2 **Challenging** yourself and others to go beyond description and assumptions to critical analysis and evaluation.
3 **Sharing** what you are learning with colleagues – to enrich understanding and enhance the quality of practice.

These essentials will help you as you apply and adapt the rich ideas and approaches in this book in your own particular context. They will also help you if you are, or are about to be, taking part in a Cambridge Professional Development Qualification (Cambridge PDQ) programme, to make the most of your programme, develop your portfolio and gain the qualification.

1 Focus
In principle

Given the multiple dimensions and demands of being a teacher, you might be tempted to try to cover 'everything' in your professional development but you will then not have the time to go beneath the surface much at all. Likewise, attending many different training events will certainly keep you very busy but it is unlikely that these will simply add up to improving your thinking and practice in sustainable and systematic ways.

Teachers who are beginning an organised programme of professional learning find that it is most helpful to select particular ideas, approaches and topics which are relevant to their own situation and their school's priorities. They can then be clear about their professional learning goals, and how their own learning contributes to improving their students' learning outcomes. They deliberately choose activities that help make sense of their practice with their students in their school and have a clear overall purpose.

It is one thing achieving focus, and another maintaining this over time. When the going gets tough, because it is difficult either to understand or become familiar with new ideas and practices, or to balance learning time with the demands of work and life, it really helps to have a mission – to know why you want to learn something as well as what that something is. Make sure that this is a purpose which you feel genuinely belongs to you and in which you have a keen interest, rather than it being something given to you or imposed on you. Articulate your focus not just by writing it down but by 'pitching' it to a colleague whose opinion you trust and taking note of their feedback.

In practice

- Plan
  What is my goal and how will I approach the activity?

  Select an approach that is new to you, but make sure that you understand the thinking behind this and that it is relevant to your students' learning. Do it for real effect, not for show.

- Monitor
  Am I making progress towards my goal; do I need to try a different approach?

  Take time during your professional development programme to review how far and well you are developing your understanding of theory and practice. What can you do to get more out of the experience, for example by discussing issues with your mentor, researching particular points, and asking your colleagues for their advice?

- Evaluate
  What went well, what could have been better, what have I learned for next time?

  Evaluation can sometimes be seen as a 'duty to perform' – like clearing up after the event – rather than the pivotal moment in learning that it really is. Evaluate not because you are told you have to; evaluate to make sense of the learning experience you have been through and what it means to you, and to plan ahead to see what you can do in the future.

This cycle of planning, monitoring and evaluation is just as relevant to you as a professional learner as to your students as learners. Be actively in charge of your learning and take appropriate actions. Make your professional development work for you. Of course your professional development programme leaders, trainers and mentors will guide and support you in your learning, but you are at the heart of your own learning experience, not on the receiving end of something that is cast in stone. Those who assist and advise you on your professional development want you and your colleagues to get the best out of the experience, and need your feedback along the way so that if necessary they can adapt and improve what they are devising.

2 Challenge

In principle

Reflection is a constructive process that helps the individual teacher to improve their thinking and practice. It involves regularly asking questions of yourself about your developing ideas and experience, and keeping track of your developing thinking, for example in a reflective journal. Reflection is continuous, rather than a one-off experience. Being honest with yourself means thinking hard, prompting yourself to go beyond your first thoughts about a new experience and to avoid taking for granted your opinions about something to which you are accustomed. Be a critical friend to yourself.

In the Cambridge PDQ Certificate in Teaching and Learning, for example, teachers take a fresh look at the concepts and processes of learning and challenge their own assumptions. They engage with theory and models of effective teaching and learning, and open their minds through observing experienced practitioners, applying new ideas in practice and listening to formative feedback from mentors and colleagues. To evidence in their assessed portfolio how they have learned from this experience, they not only present records of observed practice but also critical analysis showing understanding of how and why practices work and how they can be put into different contexts successfully.

The Cambridge PDQ syllabuses set out key questions to focus professional learning and the portfolio templates prompts to help you. These questions provide a framework for reflection. They are open-ended and will not only stimulate your thinking but lead to lively group discussion. The discipline of asking yourself and others questions such as 'Why?' 'How do we know?' 'What is the evidence?' 'What are the conditions?' leads to thoughtful and intelligent practice.

In practice

Challenge:

- Yourself, as you reflect on an experience, to be more critical in your thinking. For example, rather than simply describing what happened, analyse why it happened and its significance, and what might have happened if conditions had been different.
- Theory – by understanding and analysing the argument, and evaluating the evidence that supports the theory. Don't simply accept a theory as a given fact – be sure that you feel that the ideas make sense and that there is positive value in applying them in practice.
- Convention – the concept of 'best practice(s)' is as good as we know now, on the basis of the body of evidence, for example on the effect size of impact of a particular approach on learning outcomes (defined in the next chapter). By using an approach in an informed way and with a critical eye, you can evaluate the approach relating to your particular situation.

3 Share

In principle

Schools are such busy places, and yet teachers can feel they are working on their own for long periods because of the intensity of their workload as they focus on all that is involved in teaching their students. We know that a crucial part of our students' active learning is the opportunity to collaborate with their peers in order to investigate, create and communicate. Just so with professional learning: teachers learn best through engagement with their peers, in their own school and beyond. Discussion and interaction with colleagues, focused on learning and student outcomes, and carried out in a culture of openness, trust and respect, helps each member of the community of practice in the school clarify and sharpen their understanding and enhance their practice.

This is why the best professional learning programmes incorporate collaborative learning, and pivotal moments are designed into the programme for this to happen frequently over time: formally in guided learning sessions such as workshops and more informally in opportunities such as study group, teach meets and discussion, both face-to-face and online.

In practice

Go beyond expectations!

In the Cambridge PDQ syllabus, each candidate needs to carry out an observation of an experienced practitioner and to be observed formatively themselves by their mentor on a small number of occasions. This is the formal requirement in terms of evidence of practice within the portfolio for the qualification. The expectation is that these are not the only times that teachers will observe and be observed for professional learning purposes (rather than performance appraisal).

However, the more that teachers can observe each other's teaching, the better; sharing of practice leads to advancement of shared knowledge and understanding of aspects of teaching and learning, and development of agreed shared 'best practice'.

So:

• open your classroom door to observation
• share with your closest colleague(s) when you are trying out a fresh approach, such as an idea in this book
• ask them to look for particular aspects in the lesson, especially how students are engaging with the approach – pose an observation question
• reflect with them after the lesson on what you and they have learned from the experience – pose an evaluation question
• go and observe them as they do the same
• after a number of lessons, discuss with your colleagues how you can build on your peer observation with common purpose (for example lesson study).
• share with your other colleagues in the school what you are gaining from this collaboration and encourage them to do the same
• always have question(s) to focus observations and focus these question(s) on student outcomes.

Pathways

The short-term effects of professional development are very much centred on teachers' students. For example, the professional learning in a Cambridge PDQ programme should lead directly and quickly to changes in the ways your students learn. All teachers have this at heart – the desire to help their students learn better.

The long-term effects of professional development are more teacher-centric. During their career over, say, 30 years, a teacher may teach many thousand lessons. There are many good reasons for a teacher to keep up-to-date with pedagogy, not least to sustain their enjoyment of what they do.

Each teacher will follow their own career pathway, taking into account many factors. We do work within systems, at school and wider level, involving salary and appointment levels, and professional development can be linked to these as requirement or expectation. However, to a significant extent teachers shape their own career pathway, making decisions along the way. Their pathway is not pre-ordained; there is room for personal choice, opportunity and serendipity. It is for each teacher to judge for themselves how much they wish to venture. A teacher's professional development pathway should reflect and support this.

It is a big decision to embark on an extended programme of professional development, involving a significant commitment of hours of learning and preparation over several months. You need to be as clear as you can be about the immediate and long-term value of such a commitment. Will your programme lead to academic credit as part of a stepped pathway towards Masters level, for example?

Throughout your career, you need to be mindful of the opportunities you have for professional development. Gauge the value of options available at each particular stage in your professional life, both in terms of relevance to your current situation – your students, subject and phase focus, and school – and the future situation(s) of which you are thinking.

Understanding the impact of classroom practice on student progress

Lee Davis, Deputy Director for Education, Cambridge International

Introduction

Throughout this book, you have been encouraged to adopt a more active approach to teaching and learning and to ensure that formative assessment is embedded into your classroom practice. In addition, you have been asked to develop your students as meta-learners, such that they are able to, as the academic Chris Watkins puts it, 'narrate their own learning' and become more reflective and strategic in how they plan, carry out and then review any given learning activity.

A key question remains, however. How will you know that the new strategies and approaches you intend to adopt have made a significant difference to your students' progress and learning? What, in other words, has been the impact and how will you know?

This chapter looks at how you might go about determining this at the classroom level. It deliberately avoids reference to whole-school student tracking systems, because these are not readily available to all schools and all teachers. Instead, it considers what you can do as an individual teacher to make the learning of your students visible – both to you and anyone else who is interested in how they are doing. It does so by introducing the concept of 'effect sizes' and shows how these can be used by teachers to determine not just whether an intervention works or not but, more importantly, *how well* it works. 'Effect size' is a useful way of quantifying or measuring the size of any difference between two groups or data sets. The aim is to place emphasis on the most important aspect of an intervention or change in teaching approach – the **size of the effect** on student outcomes.

Consider the following scenario:

Over the course of a term, a teacher has worked hard with her students on understanding 'what success looks like' for any given task or activity. She has stressed the importance of everyone being clear about the criteria for success, before students embark upon the chosen task and plan their way through it. She has even got to the point where students have been co-authors of the assessment rubrics used, so that they have been fully engaged in the intended outcomes throughout and can articulate what is required before they have even started. The teacher is happy with developments so far, but has it made a difference to student progress? Has learning increased beyond what we would normally expect for an average student over a term anyway?

Here is an extract from the teacher's markbook.

Student	Sept Task	Nov Task
Katya	13	15
Maria	15	20
Joao	17	23
David	20	18
Mushtaq	23	25
Caio	25	38
Cristina	28	42
Tom	30	35
Hema	32	37
Jennifer	35	40

Figure 14.1

Before we start analysing this data, we must note the following:

* The task given in September was at the start of the term – the task in November was towards the end of the term.
* Both tasks assessed similar skills, knowledge and understanding in the student.
* The maximum mark for each was 50.
* The only variable that has changed over the course of the term is the approaches to teaching and learning by the teacher. All other things are equal.

With that in mind, looking at Figure 14.1, what conclusions might you draw as an external observer?

You might be saying something along the lines of: 'Mushtaq and Katya have made some progress, but not very much. Caio and Cristina appear to have done particularly well. David, on the other hand, appears to be going backwards!'

What can you say about the class as a whole?

Calculating effect sizes

What if we were to apply the concept of 'effect sizes' to the class results in Figure 13.1, so that we could make some more definitive statements about the impact of the interventions over the given time period? Remember, we are doing so in order to understand the size of the effect on student outcomes or progress.

Let's start by understanding how it is calculated.

An effect size is found by calculating 'the standardised mean difference between two data sets or groups'. In essence, this means we are looking for the difference between two averages, while taking into the account the spread of values (in this case, marks) around those averages at the same time.

As a formula, and from Figure 14.1, it looks like the following:

$$\text{Effect size} = \frac{\text{average class mark (after intervention)} - \text{average class mark (before intervention)}}{\text{spread (standard deviation of the class)}}$$

In words: the average mark achieved by the class *before* the teacher introduced her intervention strategies is taken away from the average mark achieved by the class *after* the intervention strategies. This is then divided by the standard deviation[1] of the class as a whole.

---

[1] The standard deviation is merely a way of expressing by how much the members of a group (in this case, student marks in the class) differ from the average value (or mark) for the group.

Inserting our data into a spreadsheet helps us calculate the effect size as follows:

	A	B	C
1	Student	September Task	November Task
2	Katya	13	15
3	Maria	15	20
4	Joao	17	23
5	David	20	18
6	Mushtaq	23	25
7	Caio	25	38
8	Cristina	28	42
9	Tom	30	35
10	Hema	32	37
11	Jennifer	35	40
12			
13	Average mark	23.8 = AVERAGE (B2:B11)	29.3 = AVERAGE (C2:C11)
14	Standard deviation	7.5 = STDEV (B2:B11)	10.1 = STDEV (C2:C11)

Figure 14.2

Therefore, the effect size for this class $= \dfrac{29.3 - 23.8}{8.8} = 0.62$

But what does this mean?

Interpreting effect sizes for classroom practice

In pure statistical terms, a 0.62 effect size means that the average student mark **after** the intervention by the teacher, is 0.62 standard deviations above the average student mark **before** the intervention.

We can state this in another way: the post-intervention average mark now exceeds 61% of the student marks previously.

Going further, we can also say that the average student mark, post-intervention, would have placed a student in the top four in the class previously. You can see this visually in Figure 14.2 where 29.3 (the class average after the teacher's interventions) would have been between Cristina's and Tom's marks in the September task.

This is good, isn't it? As a teacher, would you be happy with this progress by the class over the term?

To help understand effect sizes further, and therefore how well or otherwise the teacher has done above, let us look at how they are used in large-scale studies as well as research into educational effectiveness more broadly. We will then turn our attention to what really matters – talking about student learning.

Effect sizes in research

We know from results analyses of the Program for International Student Assessment (PISA) and the Trends in International Mathematics and Science Study (TIMMS) that, across the world, a year's schooling leads to an effect size of 0.4. John Hattie and his team at The University of Melbourne reached similar conclusions when looking at over 900 meta-analyses of classroom and whole-school interventions to improve student learning – 240 million students later, the result was an effect size of 0.4 on average for all these strategies.

What this means, then, is that any teacher achieving an effect size of greater than 0.4 is doing better than expected (than the average) over the course of a year. From our earlier example, not only are the students making better than expected progress, they are also doing so in just one term.

Here is something else to consider. In England, the distribution of GCSE grades in Maths and English have standard deviations of between 1.5 and 1.8 grades (A★, A, B, C, etc.), so an improvement of one GCSE grade represents an effect size of between 0.5 and 0.7. This means that, in the context of secondary schools, introducing a change in classroom practice of 0.62 (as the teacher achieved above) would result in an improvement of about one GCSE grade for each student in the subject.

Furthermore, for a school in which 50% of students were previously attaining five or more A★–C grades, this percentage (assuming the effect size of 0.62 applied equally across all subjects and all other things being equal) would rise to 73%.

Now, that's something worth knowing.

What next for your classroom practice? Talking about student learning

Given what we now know about 'effect sizes', what might be the practical next steps for you as a teacher?

Firstly, try calculating 'effect sizes' for yourself, using marks and scores for your students that are comparable, e.g. student performance on key skills in Maths, Reading, Writing, Science practicals, etc. Become familiar with how they are calculated so that you can then start interrogating them 'intelligently'.

Do the results indicate progress was made? If so, how much is attributable to the interventions you have introduced?

Try calculating 'effect sizes' for each individual student, in addition to your class, to make their progress visible too. To help illustrate this, let us return to the comments we were making about the progress of some students in Figure 14.1. We thought Cristina and Caio did very well and we had grave concerns about David. Individual effect sizes for the class of students would help us shed light on this further:

Student	September Task	November task	Individual Effect Size
Katya	13	15	0.22*
Maria	15	20	0.55
Joao	17	23	0.66
David	20	18	-0.22
Mushtaq	23	25	0.22
Caio	25	38	1.43
Cristina	28	42	1.54
Tom	30	35	0.55
Hema	32	37	0.55
Jennifer	35	40	0.55

* The individual 'effect size' for each student above is calculated by taking their September mark away from their November mark and then dividing by the standard deviation for the class – in this case, 8.8.

Figure 14.3

If these were your students, what questions would you now ask of yourself, of your students and even of your colleagues, to help you understand why the results are as they are and how learning is best achieved? Remember, an effect size of 0.4 is our benchmark, so who is doing better than that? Who is not making the progress we would expect?

David's situation immediately stands out, doesn't it? A negative effect size implies learning has regressed. So, what has happened, and how will we draw alongside him to find out what the issues are and how best to address them?

Why did Caio and Cristina do so well, considering they were just above average previously? Effect sizes of 1.43 and 1.54 respectively are significantly above the benchmark, so what has changed from their perspective? Perhaps they responded particularly positively to developing assessment rubrics together. Perhaps learning had sometimes been a mystery to them before, but with success criteria now made clear, this obstacle to learning had been removed.

We don't know the answers to these questions, but they would be great to ask, wouldn't they? So go ahead and ask them. Engage in dialogue with your students, and see how their own ability to discuss their learning has changed and developed. This will be as powerful a way as any of discovering whether your new approaches to teaching and learning have had an impact and it ultimately puts data, such as 'effect sizes', into context.

Concluding remarks

'Effect sizes' are a very effective means of helping you understand the impact of your classroom practice upon student progress. If you change your teaching strategies in some way, calculating 'effect sizes', for both the class and each individual student, helps you determine not just *if* learning has improved, but by *how much*.

They are, though, only part of the process. As teachers, we must look at the data carefully and intelligently in order to understand 'why'. Why did some students do better than others? Why did some not make any progress at all? Use 'effect sizes' as a starting point, not the end in itself.

Ensure that you don't do this in isolation – collaborate with others and share this approach with them. What are your colleagues finding in their classes, in their subjects? Are the same students making the same progress across the curriculum? If there are differences, what might account for them?

In answering such questions, we will be in a much better position to determine next steps in the learning process for students. After all, isn't that our primary purpose as teachers?

Acknowledgements, further reading and resources

This chapter has drawn extensively on the influential work of the academics John Hattie and Robert Coe. You are encouraged to look at the following resources to develop your understanding further:

Hattie, J. (2012) *Visible Learning for Teachers – Maximising Impact on Learning*. London and New York: Routledge.

Coe, R. (2002) *It's the Effect Size, Stupid. What effect size is and why it is important.* Paper presented at the Annual Conference of The British Educational Research Association, University of Exeter, England, 12–14 September, 2002. A version of the paper is available online on the University of Leeds website.

The Centre for Evaluation and Monitoring, University of Durham, has produced a very useful 'effect size' calculator (available from their website). Note that it also calculates a confidence interval for any 'effect size' generated. Confidence intervals are useful in helping you understand the margin for error of an 'effect size' you are reporting for your class. These are particularly important when the sample size is small, which will inevitably be the case for most classroom teachers.

Recommended reading

15

For a deeper understanding of the Cambridge approach, refer to the Cambridge International website (http://www. cambridgeinternational.org/teaching-and-learning) where you will find the following resources:

Implementing the curriculum with Cambridge: a guide for school leaders.

Developing your school with Cambridge: a guide for school leaders.

Education Briefs for a number of topics, such as active learning and bilingual education. Each brief includes information about the challenges and benefits of different approaches to teaching, practical tips, lists of resources.

Getting started with … These are interactive resources to help explore and develop areas of teaching and learning. They include practical examples, reflective questions, and experiences from teachers and researchers.

For further support around becoming a Cambridge school, visit cambridge-community.org.uk.

The resources in this section can be used as a supplement to your learning, to build upon your awareness of Primary teaching and the pedagogical themes in this series.

The English Primary Geography programme of study can be found on the UK government website.

Bourn, D., Hunt, F., Blum, F. and Lawson, H. (2016) *Primary Education for Global Learning and Sustainability.* York: Cambridge Primary Review Trust.

Higgins, S., Xiao, Z. and Katsipataki, M. (2012) *The Impact of Digital Technology on Learning: A summary for the Education Endowment Foundation.* Available at the Education Endowment Foundation website.

MacKeith, M. (2012) 'Breaking the cycle of isolation and ignorance', in T. Cotton (ed.) *Towards an Education for Social Justice.* Oxford: Peter Lang.

Oxfam (2015) *Education for Global Citizenship: A Guide for Schools.* Oxford: Oxfam.

Tyler, R. W. (1949) *Basic Principles of Curriculum and Instruction.* Chicago: University of Chicago Press.

UNDES (2015) *Transforming Our World: The 2030 Agenda for Sustainable Development.* New York: United Nations Department of Economics and Social Affairs.

Watkins, C. (2015) *Meta-Learning in Classrooms.* The SAGE Handbook of Learning. Edited by Scott D. and Hargreaves E. London: Sage Publications.

Index